Unit 7
Kindergarten Ecology
A collection of theme-related ideas and activities

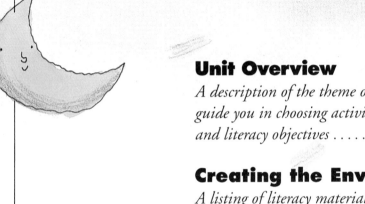

Unit Overview

Kindergarten Ecology

Theme Organization

On these pages you will find a description of the organization of this Teacher's Guide for the theme *Kindergarten Ecology.* Each theme in the *Celebrate Reading!* Kindergarten program is divided into three sections. Each section includes a variety of activities that will enhance your curriculum.

Note: A listing of *Core Literacy Activities,* included in each section, provides a weekly plan that will assist you in creating a well-balanced literacy program.

Background Information

Core Literacy Activities
A core plan for the week

Literature
Theme-related literature

Letters and Words
Activities to increase letter knowledge

Kindergarteners Read
Activities that foster reading development

Kindergarteners Write
Activities that foster writing development

Oral Language
Activities focusing on speaking and listening

Dramatic Play
Implementing dramatic play centers

Art
Creative extensions of the section topic

Music
Songs and activities related to the section topic

Across the Curriculum
Math, science, social studies, health activities

Books to Enjoy
Books related to the section topic

Section ❶

Section ❷

Section ❸

Creating the
Environment

Science Center

- Display seed packets with labels.
- Provide seeds, beans, garden soil, planters, and growth observation charts.
- Provide objects from nature, such as leaves, rocks, and pine cones, for sorting and classifying.
- Display weather charts, maps, and graphs.

The Writing Center

- Provide a variety of writing tools and construction paper for making books about the seasons.
- Display the names of the months and days of the week so children can make their own calendars and weather charts.

Music Center

- Provide on charts the words to songs that children learn during the unit.
- Encourage children to use recyclable materials they have collected, such as cardboard boxes, cardboard tubes, rubber bands, and aluminum cans with pebbles inside, for rhythm band instruments.

Social Studies Center

- Provide and display informational books, picture magazines, and photographs showing various environments around the world.
- Make available state and national park brochures.

Read a Good Book

The Library Corner

- Provide picture books related to nature, the environment, and growing things.
- Provide gardening magazines, seed and flower catalogs, and nature magazines.

Manipulative Center

- As children bring in recyclable materials, such as aluminum cans and bottle tops, encourage them to count, sort, label, and tally these items.

The theme *Kindergarten Ecology* is supported by placing literacy rich materials in the classroom. Environmental signs and labels on materials help children make sense of their environment. A focus on weather and the seasons will provide opportunities for displaying many different visual supports, such as weather and seasonal charts and various scenes from nature.

Art Center

- Provide and label materials from nature for collage making.
- Provide labeled containers for sorting recyclable art materials, such as yarn, foam pieces, and bottle tops, that children bring in to use for collage and sculpture making.
- Display color words for different colors seen in nature.
- Make available painting supplies and paints for children to create rainbows and landscape scenes.

Dramatic Play

- Materials and equipment suggestions for creating a weather station, running a flower shop, and going camping are found on pages 30, 56, and 80.

Section ❶  Seasons

Background Information

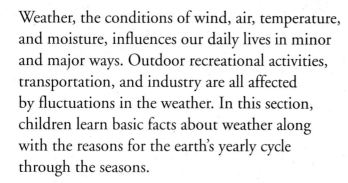

Weather, the conditions of wind, air, temperature, and moisture, influences our daily lives in minor and major ways. Outdoor recreational activities, transportation, and industry are all affected by fluctuations in the weather. In this section, children learn basic facts about weather along with the reasons for the earth's yearly cycle through the seasons.

As you guide children through this section, you may want to highlight the following concepts and vocabulary related to weather.

- *Precipitation* (snow, rain, drizzle, hail, and sleet)
  Snow forms when droplets of water in clouds freeze into ice crystals.
  Drizzle is a type of rain with very fine drops of water.
  Hail is ice and snow in the form of solid pellets.
  Sleet is a mixture of rain and snow.
- *Lightning* is a discharge of static electricity formed by violent air currents in clouds.
- *Thunder* is the sound generated by the forceful expansion of air caused by lightning.
- *Water vapor* is water in the form of invisible gas in the air.
  Dew is water vapor that has condensed into liquid.
  Frost is frozen water vapor in the form of ice crystals.
  Fog is condensed water vapor in cloudlike forms near the surface of the Earth.
- A *meteorologist* is a scientist who studies weather. Computers, satellites, and weather balloons are among the equipment used by meteorologists to forecast the weather.

and Weather

You may wish to expose children to the following vocabulary and concepts about the seasons.

- The planet Earth tilts on its *axis*, the imaginary line between the North and South Poles, as it *orbits*, or circles, the sun. One half of the year the northern end of the planet tilts toward the sun and experiences warmer temperatures, while the southern end tilts away and has colder temperatures. Seasonal changes occur as the earth continues its orbit, and the northern end tilts away from the sun, while the southern end tilts toward it.

- It takes the earth one *day* and one *night* to spin on its axis. It takes the moon one *month* to orbit the Earth. One *year* is the length of time required for the earth to orbit the sun.

Possibilities for classroom activities in this section include:

- Recording weather changes on a calendar and graphing results.
- Discussing appropriate clothing for various weather conditions.
- Discussing safety precautions during storms.
- Acting as meteorologists in dramatic play.
- Observing and reading about changes in plants and wildlife through the seasons.

Core Literacy Activities

A core activity plan for the week

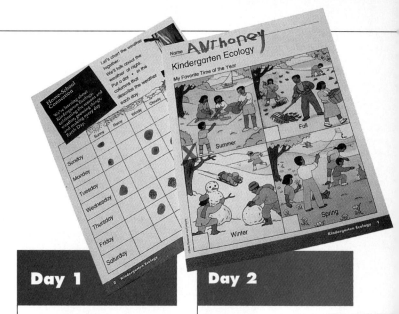

Getting Started

Engage children in an initial discussion to stimulate thinking about the weather and seasonal changes characteristic of the region in which they live. Encourage children to identify their favorite seasons on Activity Sheet 1. Have children record their favorite seasons by putting Xs in the appropriate boxes. Read Home-School Connection Sheet 2 with children; then send it home to inform family members about the theme. The weekly plan shown will assist you in creating a well-balanced literacy program. The core activities listed are designated throughout the Teacher's Guide by a blue activity square ■. Also listed are activities that take more time to complete and are especially adaptable to *full day* programs.

Throughout the Week

As you progress through your literacy program, encourage children to record daily weather changes. Set up a weather station in the dramatic play area, sing songs, recite rhymes, and converse with children. Focus on the letters *Ss, Rr,* and *Uu* and the letter/sound relationships.

Using a Four Week Plan

The average class will spend about four weeks on a unit, using the materials in one section during each of the first three weeks. The fourth week can be spent completing activities that need more time or reinforcement, rereading favorite literature, and working on the culminating unit project.

Day 1

Reading **11**
Read the Big Book

Oral Language **12**
Talk About the Story

Writing **14**
Write About Baby Bear

Full Day Extended Time Activity **17**
Make Print Pictures

Day 2

Reading **18**
Introduce the Letters *Ss*

Oral Language **13**
Reread the Story

Writing **26**
Record Information About Rainfall

Full Day Extended Time Activity **28**
Make a Birdfeeder

The Big Book

Theme-related literature

The
Bears'
Autumn

by Keizaburo Tejima

Your Ideas

_____

_____

_____

_____

_____

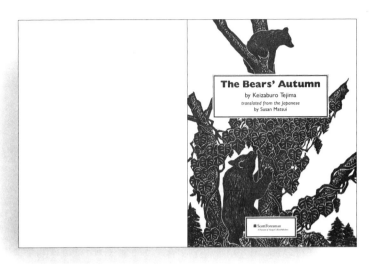

The Bears' Autumn
by Keizaburo Tejima
translated from the Japanese
by Susan Matsui

ScottForesman

The autumn mountains of Hokkaido, the northern island of Japan, are aflame with beautiful colors.

2

The clear sky seems to spread out forever. The chilly autumn wind comes blowing, and a jay calls.

3

Something dark is moving about in the forest. There's a little one, too. It's a mother and baby brown bear. They're eating something to fatten up for their long winter sleep.

4

5

Read the Big Book

Core Activity

LITERACY OBJECTIVES

The child listens to a variety of literature to increase background information, language of books, and attention span; attends to adult models of literacy behaviors.

- Display the Big Book, *The Bears' Autumn*, and read the title and author's name.
- Invite children to look at the illustrations on the cover and the title page. Explain that the story takes place in a forest in Japan. Locate Japan on a globe or map.
- You might wish to discuss briefly the seasonal changes that take place in a forest in autumn, such as trees turning color and losing leaves, and animals storing food for winter.
- Ask children to share their knowledge about bears and how bears prepare for winter.
- Encourage children to make predictions about what might happen in the story based on the illustrations, the title, and their knowledge about bears and autumn.

Talk About the Story

Core Activity

Mother and Baby Bear are eating tasty, ripe wild grapes.

LITERACY OBJECTIVE

The child asks appropriate questions and makes appropriate comments about text and pictures.

MATERIALS

paper, drawing materials

- Invite children to comment on the story. How do they feel about Baby Bear? What does the story make children think about?
- Provide paper, pencils, and crayons and invite children to write/draw about the story.
- Give children time to share and discuss their ideas and pictures about the story with each other.

Baby Bear with his light body is a better tree-climber than his mother. "I wonder what I can see from the top of this tree."

Observing the Child

Children's understandings of print and word can be observed in conjunction with Big Book activities. During rereadings of the Big Book, ask a child to

- track print from top to bottom and left to right as you reread.
- identify and frame a high-frequency word with their hands.
- point to and identify sentence punctuation.
- identify a sentence by pointing to the first word and ending punctuation.

From high up in the tree, Baby Bear sees sparkling white mountains in the distance. And he sees a beautiful river. "I'm going to fish for salmon in that river tonight," thinks Baby Bear excitedly. It would be his very first trip to fish for salmon.

When the sunset fades and moonlight shines on the forest, Mother and Baby Bear come to the edge of the river.
"Will they come? Will they really come?" asks Baby Bear.
"Yes, of course they will."

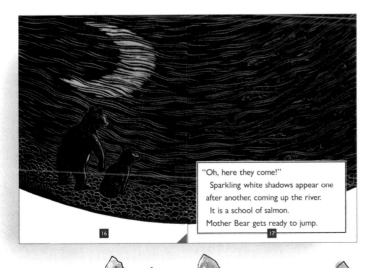

"Oh, here they come!"
Sparkling white shadows appear one after another, coming up the river.
It is a school of salmon.
Mother Bear gets ready to jump.

Reread the Story

Core Activity

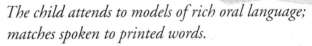

LITERACY OBJECTIVES

The child attends to models of rich oral language; matches spoken to printed words.

MATERIALS

audiocassette tape Kindergarten Ecology—*side 1* **KIT** , *blank word cards, markers*

- Invite children to listen carefully to the words that the author has chosen to describe the mountains and the river. Share and discuss how this language adds to the reader's understanding and enjoyment of the story. Provide the audiocassette tape for additional listening opportunities.
- Page through the story, focusing on the dialogue between Baby Bear and Mama Bear. Invite children to read the words with you as you point to them.
- Write the words *bear*, *forest*, *river*, *fish*, and *moon* on word cards. Use the word cards to review initial consonants, print direction, and word boundaries. Invite volunteers to match the word cards to the text as you read.

Write About Baby Bear

Core Activity

LITERACY OBJECTIVES

The child uses various forms of writing; the child makes progress toward writing readable text.

MATERIALS

paper, pencils, crayons

- Invite children to brainstorm other adventures for Baby Bear. Record ideas on the chalkboard.
- Have each child select one of the adventures for a storybook.
- Encourage children to record their stories through drawing and writing, using a combination of artwork and print on each page.
- When books are finished, invite children to exchange books with a friend or share their books by reading to one another.

Kindergarten Word *will*

- Read children the following sentences from the Big Book:

"Will they come?"
"Will they really come?"
"Yes, of course they will."

Invite children to match the word card *will* to the word in the story.

- On chart paper, write several sentences with children's names as shown below. Brainstorm endings for each sentence, then read them together.

Tessa will_____.
Domingo will_____.

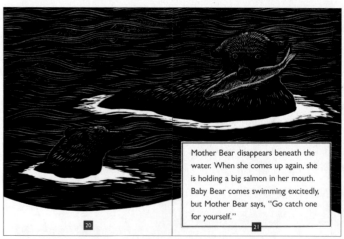

Mother Bear disappears beneath the water. When she comes up again, she is holding a big salmon in her mouth. Baby Bear comes swimming excitedly, but Mother Bear says, "Go catch one for yourself."

Baby Bear chases the salmon as fast as he can. But try as he might, he can't catch them.
"That's it. I'll try diving as Mommy did."

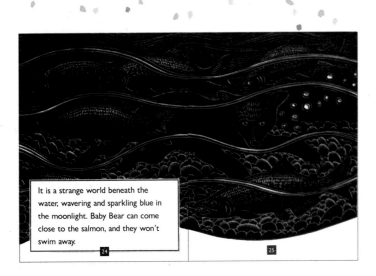

It is a strange world beneath the water, wavering and sparkling blue in the moonlight. Baby Bear can come close to the salmon, and they won't swim away.

24

25

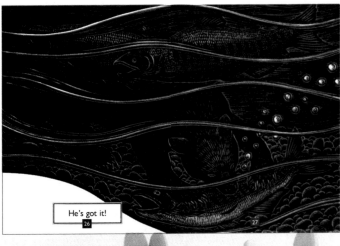

He's got it!

26

27

Create a Sparkle Poster

Optional Activity

LITERACY OBJECTIVES

The child matches spoken to printed words; attends to adult models of writing.

MATERIALS

butcher paper, glue, glitter, writing materials

- Draw children's attention to these phrases in the Big Book:

"sparkling white mountains"
"sparkling white shadows"
"wavering and sparkling blue"
"moonlight sparkles on the water"

- Explain that when something sparkles, it shines and looks bright. Encourage children to think of things that sparkle and write a list on the board.

Snow sparkles.
Glitter sparkles.
Diamonds sparkle.
Gold sparkles.

- Place a large sheet of butcher paper on the floor. Invite children to use glue and glitter to make the paper sparkle. Then have children copy the sentences from the board onto the sparkle poster.

Learn About Cycles of Time

Optional Activity

LITERACY OBJECTIVE

The child is interested in a variety of literary genres.

MATERIALS

books about telling time, day and night, and the seasons; timer

- Set a timer or use a sandglass timer, inviting children to watch as the timer ticks off the seconds or the sand passes from one chamber to another.
- Draw children's attention to the classroom clock and the classroom calendar. Explain that timers, clocks, and calendars show that time is passing.
- Write the following words on the chalkboard or on word cards: *month, hour, year, season, week, day.* Help children put the list in order, from the shortest to the longest time duration.
- Talk about the changes that take place in nature from day to night and from season to season.
- Provide books and pictures on the subject for children to read and examine.

Baby Bear climbs out of the river, proudly holding a fine, big salmon in his mouth. He shakes himself all over.

28   29

Baby Bear eats salmon for the first time in his life. How good it tastes, the salmon he has caught all by himself! On the river behind him, the moonlight sparkles and swirls,

30   31

and becomes a big, big fish. The lively little bear decides to catch it.

32   33

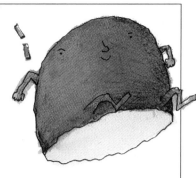

Make Print Pictures

Extended Time Activity

LITERACY OBJECTIVES

The child can differentiate between pictures and text; knows that letters make words; attends to and contributes to a print-rich environment by making books and writing stories.

MATERIALS

wooden blocks, cork, spools, potatoes, paint in shallow trays or saucers, paper

Fine Arts **Multicultural**

- Tell children that the illustrations in *The Bears' Autumn* are not paintings, but Japanese woodcuts.
- Explain that woodcuts are made from blocks of wood. First the artist uses sharp tools to make pictures or designs in the wood. Next ink is spread over the wood and the block is pressed onto paper. When the block is removed, it leaves an ink design on the paper.
- Demonstrate for children by carving a simple picture or shape on the end of a peeled potato. Dip the potato in paint and press it on paper to show children how the raised part of the potato leaves its shape on the page.
- Invite children to make their own print pictures. Provide a variety of materials for printmaking, such as potatoes, wooden blocks, cork, and spools.

"Mommy, look! There's a great big fish in here!"
"Silly little bear, that's just the moonlight on the water!" Mother Bear says, with a gentle smile.

When the moon has set and the night sky is full of stars, Baby Bear is back in the den, sleeping by his mother's side.

He has a dream about a big, big fish. Twinkling like the stars, the fish swims slowly through the night sky.

Letters and Words

Activities to increase letter knowledge

Introduce the Letters Ss

Core Activity

The activities suggested on this page should be used after children have learned letter names and have had multiple experiences with letters in environmental print and literature.

LITERACY OBJECTIVES
The child identifies letters of the alphabet; identifies letter/sound correspondences; uses initial letters as clues to word recognition.

MATERIALS
classroom alphabet picture cards **KIT** *, picture cards* **KIT** *, lap-sized chalkboards* **KIT** *, manipulative letters* **KIT** *, or available picture cards and manipulative letters (Adapt activity for use with your materials.)*

Recognize the Letter
- Write the word *sun* on the chalkboard and tell children that the word *sun* begins with the letter *s*.
- Circle or underline the letter.
- Point to and name the letters *Ss* on the classroom alphabet picture card.
- Write the letters on the chalkboard, inviting children to trace the letters in the air with their fingers.
- Encourage small groups of children to write the letters on lap-sized chalkboards.
- Have children identify *Ss* manipulative letters and use them as models for their own writing.
- Invite children to form the letters *S* and *s* with clay. Provide foam trays filled with sand in which children can form letters.

Hear the Sound for the Letter

- Point to and identify the key word picture of a sun on the classroom alphabet picture card.
- Say the word *sun* for children, emphasizing the s sound at the beginning of the word.
- As children say the word with you, draw attention to how the sound is formed in the mouth.
- Have children listen as you say the following words. Ask them to touch their knees when the word begins with the same sound they hear at the beginning of the word *sun*.

salt	*say*	*peach*	*soft*	*wagon*	*zipper*
suit	*some*	*hen*	*side*	*sell*	*Sam*

- Have children identify the picture cards that begin with the s sound – seal, socks, soap, and soup.
- Invite children to pantomime these actions involving *s*: *sit*, *sail* a boat, pet a kitten's *soft* fur, *sew* a button, *sip* fruit juice, *saw* wood, and count to *six*.
- Brainstorm other action words that are related to summer and springtime, such as *skate*, *slide*, and *swim*.

Relate the Letter with the Sound

- Write the word *summer* on the chalkboard. Invite children to brainstorm s words that remind them of summer, such as *swimming*, *sunshine*, *suntan*, *sand*, and *swimsuit*. Children may enjoy making a summer mural, including words from the list in their drawing and labeling them on their artwork. If it is winter, make a snow scene.
- Although the word *spring* begins with a blend, children will identify the initial consonant in the word as *s*.

Just for Fun

Make Sun Prints

Early on a sunny day, provide large, brightly colored pieces of construction paper. Invite children to place various objects, such as leaves, container lids, bottle tops, barrettes, or hair ribbons on the paper in a sunny spot outside. If it is a windy day, light objects could be held down with small pieces of tape. Leave the paper in the sun until the late afternoon. When children remove the objects, they will be amazed to discover the patterns created by the sun fading the color of exposed parts of the paper.

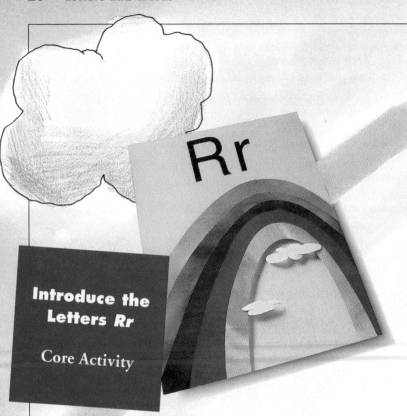

Introduce the Letters *Rr*

Core Activity

The activities suggested on this page should be used after children have learned letter names and have had multiple experiences with letters in environmental print and literature.

LITERACY OBJECTIVES

The child identifies letters of the alphabet; identifies letter/sound correspondences; uses initial letters as clues to word recognition.

MATERIALS

classroom alphabet picture cards **KIT** *, picture cards* **KIT** *, lap-sized chalkboards* **KIT** *, manipulative letters* **KIT** *, or available picture cards and manipulative letters (Adapt activity for use with your materials.)*

Recognize the Letter

- Write the word *rainbow* on the chalkboard and tell children that the word *rainbow* begins with the letter *r*.
- Circle or underline the letter.
- Point to and name the letters *Rr* on the classroom alphabet picture card.
- Write the letters on the chalkboard, inviting children to trace the letters in the air with their fingers.
- Encourage small groups of children to write the letters on lap-sized chalkboards.
- Have children identify *Rr* manipulative letters and use them as models for their own writing.
- Provide a collection of red pencils, red markers, and red crayons for children. Invite them to write several capital and lower-case letters in red.

Hear the Sound for the Letter

- Point to and identify the key word picture of a rainbow on the classroom alphabet picture card.
- Say the word *rainbow* for children, emphasizing the r sound at the beginning of the word.
- As children say the word with you, draw attention to how the sound is formed in the mouth.
- Have children listen as you say the following words. Ask them to rub their hands when the word begins with the same sound they hear at the beginning of the word *rainbow*.

rug	*rake*	*dig*	*round*	*ride*	*gift*
mud	*jeep*	*rip*	*road*	*hook*	*Randy*

- Have children identify the picture cards that begin with the r sound–rabbit, radio, ring, and rooster.

Relate the Letter with the Sound

- Invite a small group or the whole class to play "Round N' Roll Ball." One child stands in a circle with a large ball, closes his or her eyes, turns around in place a few times, then rolls the ball toward the children in the outer circle. Whomever the ball reaches must name a word beginning with *r*, which you record on the chalkboard or a chart. The player who names a word takes a turn in the circle. Play continues in the same manner. As you add each word, encourage children to read the growing list along with you.
- Read Robert Kalan's *Rain* (Greenwillow, 1978). Discuss how the word *rain* is used in the art and invite children to read the book with partners.

Introduce the Letters *Uu*

Core Activity

The activities suggested on this page should be used after children have learned letter names and have had multiple experiences with letters in environmental print and literature.

LITERACY OBJECTIVES

The child identifies letters of the alphabet; identifies letter/sound correspondences; uses initial letters as clues to word recognition.

MATERIALS

classroom alphabet picture cards **KIT** *, picture cards* **KIT** *, lap-sized chalkboards* **KIT** *, manipulative letters* **KIT** *, or available picture cards and manipulative letters (Adapt activity for use with your materials.)*

Recognize the Letter

- Write the word *umbrella* on the chalkboard and tell children that the word *umbrella* begins with the letter *u*.
- Circle or underline the letter.
- Point to and name the letters *Uu* on the classroom alphabet picture card.
- Write the letters on the chalkboard, inviting children to trace the letters in the air with their fingers.
- Encourage small groups of children to write the letters on lap-sized chalkboards.
- Have children identify *Uu* manipulative letters and use them as models for their own writing.
- Invite children to use fingerpaints to make the letters *U* and *u* or to practice writing the letters on paper.

Hear the Sound for the Letter

- Point to and identify the key word picture of an *umbrella* on the classroom alphabet picture card.
- Say the word *umbrella* for children, emphasizing the u sound at the beginning of the word.
- As children say the word with you, draw attention to how the sound is formed in the mouth.
- Tell children that the letter *u* is a vowel and that they will be learning about vowel letters as they discover more about reading and writing. If children are curious, explain that the letter can make two different sounds in a word. The following words demonstrate the long and short pronunciation of the letter *u* in the initial position.

unit	*usual*	*utensil*	*uniform*
up	*under*	*umpire*	*uncle*

- Have children identify the picture cards that begin with the u sound–underwear and unicorn.
- Invite children to pantomime the following actions: jump *up*, *unbutton* a coat, look *under* a table, make a *U-turn*, and play the *ukulele*.

Relate the Letter with the Sound

- Invite children to make umbrellas using construction paper. Add popcorn kernel rain. Have children decorate the umbrellas with the letter *u*. Then, as you create and narrate a story about a walk, have children hold their umbrellas *up* or *down* as the weather in the story changes.
- Write the word *under* on a word card. Open an umbrella and place it on the floor. Pass the word card to a child and tell the child to locate and place an object found in the classroom *under* the umbrella.

Kindergarteners Read

Activities that foster reading development

Introduce Child-Sized Big Books

Core Activity

Read Little Celebrations Book

Core Activity

LITERACY OBJECTIVES

The child reads books emergently; demonstrates comprehension through re-enacting stories in dramatic play and other forms; demonstrates comprehension by retelling stories and expository text.

MATERIALS

child-sized versions of The Bears' Autumn, *audiocassette tape* Kindergarten Ecology– side 1* **KIT** *, bear puppet* **KIT**

- Introduce the child-sized versions of *The Bears' Autumn* and invite children to compare the covers to the Big Book to confirm that it is the same story.
- Encourage children to read along as they listen to the audiocassette tape of *The Bears' Autumn*.
- Invite pairs of children to take turns "reading" the story and using the bear puppet to act out the actions. Because this story does not lend many supports to the beginning reader, children will talk through the story using the pictures rather than read the text conventionally.
- Children might also use the bear puppet to retell the story to a friend or classroom visitor.

LITERACY OBJECTIVES

The child makes progress in moving toward conventional reading of print; identifies rhyming words; uses syntax, context, phonics clues, picture clues, and memory to help identify words; uses initial letters as clues to word recognition.

MATERIALS

In My Desert *by Pat Mora*

For Shared Reading

- Invite children to discuss the cover. Have them suggest where the setting of this book might be.
- Read the title. Do children know where the setting of the book is now? Encourage children to share what they know about deserts and to predict what things they might see in this book.
- Read the book aloud, emphasizing the rhythm and repetition.
- Reread the book, inviting children to point to the repeated word on each page. Can they also find the two pairs of rhyming words—*bloom* and *zoom, stay* and *play*?

For Emergent Reading

• After placing multiple copies of the book in the library corner, encourage children to read the books alone, to partners, or to a classroom visitor.

• Remind children that they can use picture clues, beginning letters, and their memories to help them read.

Respond to the Book

• Invite children to tell what they liked or didn't like about this book.

• Have children seen any of the pictured plants or animals before? If so, where? when? was it in the spring?

• Children might enjoy using the pattern in the book to write about plants and animals that they see where they live in the spring.

Observing the Child

When observing children during independent reading activities, note which children

• choose books they can read comfortably.

• "pretend" read in their own words.

• use picture clues to predict words.

• use the print and not just the pictures to interpret the text.

• read conventionally.

Kindergarteners Write

Activities that foster writing development

Write About Rain

Core Activity

Write About a Favorite Activity

Core Activity

LITERACY OBJECTIVES
The child writes for a variety of purposes; participates in collaborative writing activities.

MATERIALS
clear glass jar, permanent marker, ruler, writing materials

- Read books such as *Rain: Causes and Effects* by Philip Steele (Franklin Watts, 1991) and invite children to talk about experiences they have had in the rain. Discuss how rain affects the environment.
- Have children write about or draw pictures showing their experiences in the rain on raindrop-shaped paper.
- If appropriate to your situation, make a rain gauge. Use an indelible marker and a ruler to mark inches or centimeters on the outside of a large glass jar. Place the jar outside.
- After the first rainfall, let children help you read the gauge to determine how much rain has fallen.
- Have children watch as you record the results of each rainfall on a graph. Keep track of the rain that falls during a week or a month.

LITERACY OBJECTIVES
The child uses various forms of writing; attends to and contributes to a print-rich environment by making books and writing stories.

MATERIALS
Activity Sheets 3-4, drawing/writing materials

- Invite children to read Activity Sheet 3 with you, identifying the seasonal activities shown on the page.
- Read the names of the months, pointing to each one, encouraging children to repeat the name with you.
- In the space provided, have children write about or draw their favorite things to do during different months of the year.
- Invite children to read Activity Sheet 4 with you. Discuss the picture and have children suggest what season the poem is describing.
- Talk about how birds and other animals keep warm in the winter. Encourage children to compare the ways they keep warm to the ways animals do.

Use a Calendar to Record Weather

Core Activity

LITERACY OBJECTIVE
The child attends to adult models of writing.

MATERIALS
radio, word cards sunny, cloudy, rainy, windy **KIT**, *blank cards, calendar, writing materials*

- Tune in a weather station on a portable radio and invite children to listen to various weather reports for two or three days.
- Show children the word cards *sunny, cloudy, rainy,* and *windy,* pointing to the words as you read them aloud.
- Provide blank cards and invite children to draw pictures to accompany the weather words on the cards. Children can take turns matching their pictures to the appropriate word cards.
- Display a calendar for the month in a prominent place in the classroom at a height accessible to children.
- Encourage children to keep a daily record of the weather on the calendar by writing one or two weather words for each day, using the word cards as models. Children may also wish to display a picture card depicting the day's weather.
- When the calendar is complete, discuss how many days were sunny, how many days were cloudy, and so on.

sunny

rainy

Oral Language

Activities focusing on speaking and listening

Make a Birdfeeder

Extended Time Activity

Talk About the Seasons

Core Activity

LITERACY OBJECTIVES

The child takes turns appropriately when engaged in conversation; responds to literal, inferential, and experiential questions; attends to adult models of literacy behaviors.

MATERIALS
chart paper, marker, drawing materials

- Write the words *Winter, Spring, Summer,* and *Fall* (or *Autumn*) on a chart.
- Involve children in a discussion of seasonal activities and appropriate clothing for each season, and record children's thoughts on the chart.
- Invite children to draw pictures of themselves in their favorite seasons, wearing the appropriate clothes and engaging in a seasonal activity.
- Have children write or dictate captions for their pictures and share them with the class.

LITERACY OBJECTIVES
The child listens to a variety of literature to increase background information, language of books, and attention span; uses increased vocabulary throughout the year.

MATERIALS
picture books, paper towel tubes, peanut butter, toasted oat cereal

- Read books such as *Has Winter Come?* by Wendy Watson (Collins, 1978) or *First Comes Spring* by Anne Rockwell (HarperCollins, 1985) as a lead-in to a discussion about how animals prepare for the different seasons.
- Ask children to recall what animals they see during the winter months and how they think these animals get their food.
- Talk about how animals find and collect food during the fall months so they have extra stored for the winter, when food is harder to find. Point out that in the spring, animals are hungry and are very active in searching for food.
- Invite children working in groups to make birdfeeders. Cut paper towel tubes in half and have children spread peanut butter on them.
- Fill a shallow tray with toasted oat cereal and have children coat the peanut-buttered rolls with the cereal.
- Hang the feeders outside a classroom window or outside a window at home where children can observe and talk about the activities of birds that come to feed.

Make Weather Books

Extended Time Activity

LITERACY OBJECTIVES

The child uses increasingly complex oral language attending to the structural elements of language (syntax) appropriate for age, language background, and dialect.

MATERIALS

writing materials, paper

Different Days

Rainy rainy day
Rainy rainy day
We'll all get wet
On a rainy rainy day.

Sunny sunny day
Sunny sunny day
We'll all go swimming
On a sunny sunny day.

Snowy snowy day
Snowy snowy day
We'll all go sledding
On a snowy snowy day.

Icy icy day
Icy icy day
We'll all go skating
On an icy icy day.

Frosty frosty day
Frosty frosty day
We'll freeze our noses
On a frosty frosty day.

by Sonja Dunn

- Read the poem aloud. Then read one verse at a time, inviting children to join in as they are able.
- Divide the class into four groups, assigning each group a verse. Invite children to create hand or body motions to accompany the verse. The entire class can recite and act out the last verse together.
- Provide each child with papers that say:
    A. *On a rainy day*
       I like to _____.
    B. *On a sunny day*
       I like to _____.
    C. *On a snowy day*
       I like to _____.
- Encourage children to fill in the blanks and illustrate each page.
- Staple the pages together to form a three-page book and invite children to share their books with the class.

Dramatic Play

Implementing dramatic play centers

**Set Up
a Weather
Station**

Extended Time
Activity

**WEATHER STATION
EQUIPMENT AND MATERIALS**

*table
chairs
classroom window
containers for water
indoor and outdoor thermometers
barometer
maps*

LITERACY MATERIALS

*weather maps
charts
weather signs
pencils and other writing tools
protractors, compasses, rulers
Blackline Master 1*

Observing weather and seasonal changes often becomes a part of the daily routine in kindergarten. After discussing the weather each day, invite children to predict what they think the weather will be like the next day. Encourage children to watch a weather report on television and then follow up with a class discussion the following day.

- Listen to a weather report on the radio so that children understand the concept of predicting weather.
- Make a list of reasons people might want to predict the weather, such as planning for a picnic or trip or dressing appropriately for the day.
- Invite children to suggest what they would include in a classroom weather station, such as thermometers, charts, graphs for recording weather, and maps.
- Set up a weather station near a window for outdoor observation.
- Suggest some experiments for children to conduct, such as melting ice cubes on a sunshine-filled windowsill and in a darker location; placing thermometers in cups of warm and cold water and then comparing the temperatures.
- Display commercial maps on walls and invite children to make their own maps.
- Invite children to look at cloud formations and record sightings on cloud-watch charts.
- Have children make weekly sun/cloud/rain/wind charts to record daily weather changes.

- Encourage children to make signs for the weather station, such as *Weather Alert, Weather Bulletin, Weather Forecast, Pollution* or *Ozone Alert.*
- Provide a large Weather Forecast chart where all forecasters can record their prediction for the next day's weather.
- Provide rulers, protractors, compasses and other adultlike writing tools for use in charting and graphing on large sheets of paper.
- Invite forecasters to interview classmates to determine how many were prepared for the day's weather and dressed accordingly.
- Provide Blackline Master 1, Weather Map, and encourage children to write temperatures and symbols for weather conditions across the country.

Art

Creative extensions of the section topic

Paint With Rain

Optional Activity

LITERACY OBJECTIVES

The child participates in pleasurable literature experiences; follows oral directions.

MATERIALS

large paper plates, powder tempera paint, water-filled spray bottles

- Read *Weather Watch–Rain* by Philip Steele (Franklin Watts, 1991), discuss the photographs, and ask children to share experiences they have had with rain.
- If feasible, invite children to look out the window on a rainy day and discuss the effects rain has on the way we view objects. For example, a swing may look blurry, a slide may look runny, or a light may look dull.

- Have children sprinkle small amounts of powder tempera paint on paper plates. Invite children to "rain" on their pictures by misting them with a spray bottle.
- Encourage children to discuss how the "rain" has changed the paints and the designs the water has created.
- Extend the activity by having children name and discuss other ways in which rain affects things around us.

Make Leaf Prints

Optional Activity

LITERACY OBJECTIVES

The child engages freely in conversation in varied situations; the child attends to others when they are speaking.

MATERIALS

poster paints, medium-sized paintbrushes, white paper, newspaper

- Involve children in a discussion of some of the changes that take place out-of-doors in the springtime, such as warming temperatures and the budding of flowers and leaves.
- Invite children to collect fresh spring leaves in a variety of shapes and sizes, or bring an assortment of leaves into class. (Leaves with well-defined veins work best.)
- Cover a table with newspaper and demonstrate how to brush paint on a leaf until it is completely covered, then place the leaf between two pieces of white paper and press.
- Carefully remove the top sheet and the leaf to reveal the colored leaf print.
- Invite children to use a variety of leaves and bright colors to create prints. The prints can be displayed on a spring bulletin board.

Music

Songs and activities related to the section topic

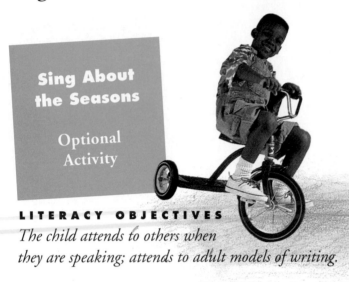

Sing About the Seasons

Optional Activity

LITERACY OBJECTIVES

The child attends to others when they are speaking; attends to adult models of writing.

MATERIALS

audiocassette tape Kindergarten Ecology—*side 2* **KIT** , *chart paper, marker*

Fine Arts

"What Shall We Do When We All Go Out?"

• Listen to the words of the song on the audiocassette tape.

• Write the words to the song on chart paper. Finger-point the words as the song is spoken as a chant.

• Encourage children to sing each verse of the song and discuss the seasons and activities mentioned.

• Make a list of other seasonal activities enjoyed by children. Sing about these activities as well, adding new verses to the song.

Dramatize a Song

Optional Activity

LITERACY OBJECTIVE

The child demonstrates comprehension through re-enacting stories in dramatic play and other forms.

MATERIALS

audiocassette tape Kindergarten Ecology—*side 2* **KIT**

• Sing the song "What Shall We Do When We All Go Out?" several times until children are familiar with the words.

• Encourage children to name each of the activities mentioned in the song and practice pantomiming the activities.

• Play the audiocassette tape for children and invite them to pantomime the words and sing along with the song.

• Encourage children to pantomime their favorite activities while the class tries to identify them.

What Shall We Do When We All Go Out?

What shall we do when we all go out, All go
out, All go out, What shall we do when we
all go out, When we all go out to play?

We will ride our three-wheel bikes,
Three-wheel bikes, three-wheel bikes,
We will ride our three-wheel bikes
When we all go out to play.

We will skate on our roller skates,
Roller skates, roller skates,
We will skate on our roller skates
When we all go out to play.

We will see-saw up and down,
Up and down, up and down,
We will see-saw up and down
When we all go out to play.

Across the Curriculum

Math, science, social studies, health activities

Learn About Sun and Color

Core Activity

LITERACY OBJECTIVES

The child follows oral directions; responds to literal, inferential, and experiential questions.

MATERIALS

large rocks, white and black paint

Science

- Talk about the warmth of the sun. Invite children to think of how the sun feels on their skin in the springtime or how a slide feels on a hot summer day.
- Distribute rocks to groups of children. Have each group paint one rock white and one black.
- Place white and black rocks on a sunny window ledge or in a sunny spot on the playground.
- After an hour, invite children to touch the rocks and tell which feel warmer, the black or white ones.
- Talk about how some things heat up more easily than others in the sun. Explain that the white rocks stay cooler because they reflect the sun's rays, while the black rocks soak up the sun's rays and become warm.
- Ask children what they would wear on a hot day in order to stay cool, a dark shirt or a light one.

Dress for Success

Optional Activity

LITERACY OBJECTIVE

The child participates in collaborative reading activities.

MATERIALS

articles of clothing

Health

- Set up a dress-up center that contains fall, winter, spring, and summer clothing, such as hats, light coats, mittens, snow pants, boots, umbrellas, slickers, shorts, swimsuits, T-shirts, and sunglasses.
- Lead children in a discussion about seasons, pointing out that to stay healthy we need to dress appropriately for each season.
- Have children listen as you read a weather bulletin; for example, *Good Morning! It is Tuesday, July 7, and we have some hot news for you today. We expect the temperature to reach 95° today, with plenty of sunshine.*
- Invite volunteers to choose clothing from the display that would be comfortable and healthy if the weather bulletin were real. Have volunteers "dress up" in the clothes chosen and explain their choices.
- Encourage pairs of children to make up their own weather bulletins and present them to the class.

Make a Seasons Mobile

Extended Time Activity

LITERACY OBJECTIVE
The child listens to a variety of literature to increase background information, language of books, and attention span.

MATERIALS
hangers, string, paper clips, writing/drawing materials

Science

- Read books about seasons such as *My Favorite Time of Year* by Susan Pearson (Harper & Row, 1988) or *Caps, Hats, Socks, and Mittens* by Louise Borden (Scholastic, 1989).
- Encourage children to talk about the changes that take place during each season and how the weather affects their activities.
- Invite children to draw pictures of activities they enjoy participating in for each of the seasons. Have children attach these pictures to paper clips hanging from a hanger, ordering them in the proper time sequence.
- Discuss the season mobiles with children, commenting on activities, time sequence, and seasonal differences.

Books to Enjoy

Books related to the section topic

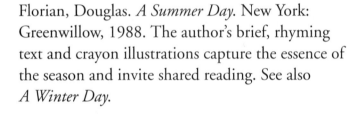

Borden, Louise. *Caps, Hats, Socks, and Mittens.* Il. by Lillian Hoban. New York: Scholastic, 1989. This delightful book, written in rhyme, highlights the changing seasons.

Domanske, Janina. *Spring Is.* New York: Greenwillow, 1976. This brief romp through the seasons inspires children to think of their own adjectives to describe their favorite times of the year.

Downing, Julie. *White Snow, Blue Feather.* New York: Bradbury, 1989. The sensitive illustrations in this book show the delights of nature that are found in the snow.

Ehlert, Lois. *Red Leaf, Yellow Leaf.* New York: Harcourt Brace Jovanovich, 1991. The well known author/illustrato combines art and photographs to create a sensational book about nature.

Florian, Douglas. *A Summer Day.* New York: Greenwillow, 1988. The author's brief, rhyming text and crayon illustrations capture the essence of the season and invite shared reading. See also *A Winter Day.*

Hirschi, Ron. *Fall.* Photographs by Thomas D. Mangelson. New York: Dutton, 1991. This collection of beautiful photographs shows animals in their mountain environment in the fall.

Kalan, Robert. *Rain.* Il. by Donald Crews. New York: Greenwillow, 1978. Rain falls on every page of this book but there's a rainbow at the end.

Keats, Ezra Jack. *The Snowy Day.* New York: Viking, 1962. The classic Caldecott Medal winner continues to delight readers with its simplicity and design.

Maass, Robert. *When Autumn Comes.* New York: Holt, 1990. The beauty of the fall season in northern New England is displayed in this book.

McCully, Emily Arnold. *First Snow.* New York: Harper & Row, 1988. This wordless picture book about a mouse family's winter outing will generate conversation about winter activities.

Pearson, Susan. *My Favorite Time of Year.* Il. by John Wallner. New York: Harper & Row, 1988. A family experiences the joys of each season as they watch the leaves turn, button-up for winter, and spot the first robin.

Rockwell, Anne. *First Comes Spring.* New York: HarperCollins, 1985, 1991. Rockwell's family of bears stays busy throughout the year.

Rogers, Paul. *What Will the Weather Be Like Today?* Il. by Kazuko. New York: Greenwillow, 1990. The rhyming text in this book gives the beginning reader a clear understanding of weather.

Spohn, Kate. *Clementine's Winter Wardrobe.* New York: Orchard Books, 1989. Children will enjoy choosing from the array of winter clothing displayed as Clementine gets ready for winter.

Steele, Philip. *Weather Watch—Snow: Causes and Effects.* New York: Franklin Watts, 1991. The photographs in this book illustrate facts about snow. See also *Weather Watch—Rain* by the same author.

Watson, Wendy. *Has Winter Come?* New York: Collins, 1978. A woodchuck family experiences the sights, sounds, and smells of winter as they gather food, roast pears, and make hot cider.

Section ❷

Growing

Background Information

Many children give flowers to their teacher as a token of appreciation and affection. In this section, teachers turn the tables and give children some "blossoms of knowledge"–the budding knowledge of plant life and its interconnection with other living things in our world.

In the section *Growing Things,* concepts presented may include the following:

- Plants manufacture their food with *chlorophyll,* a chemical that traps energy from the sun. This energy is used to combine water and carbon dioxide in a process called *photosynthesis* to make simple sugars. Mineral salts, a plant's other food requirement, are absorbed through its roots from soil.
- *Oxygen* is a by-product of photosynthesis and is released by plants into the air through their leaves. Plants therefore add to the storehouse of oxygen available for animals and humans.

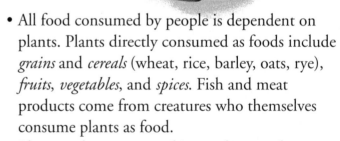

- All food consumed by people is dependent on plants. Plants directly consumed as foods include *grains* and *cereals* (wheat, rice, barley, oats, rye), *fruits, vegetables,* and *spices.* Fish and meat products come from creatures who themselves consume plants as food.
- Plants and trees are used in products such as *furniture, paper, clothing,* and *medicines.*
- Types of plants include *fungi, ferns, mosses, conifers* (trees with cones such as pine and spruce), *deciduous trees* (trees that lose their leaves in winter), *flowering plants, grasses,* and *cacti.*
- Most plants are pollinated by insects or winds which transfer *pollen* from one plant to another. After fertilization, the plant produces fruit containing seeds.
- The major types of vegetative land areas are *deserts, forests,* and *grasslands.*

Things

Possible classroom activities for this section include . . .

- Observing plants and trees on a nature walk.
- Visiting a nursery, greenhouse, conservatory, or nature center to learn more about plants and trees.
- Planting a variety of seeds in the classroom and comparing their growth.
- Learning about types of plants and trees that grow in various parts of the world.
- Identifying plants we use as food.
- Learning about the life cycle of plants.
- Learning that foods grow above or in the ground; on vines, stalks, bushes, and trees.

Core Literacy Activities

A core activity plan for the week

Getting Started

In this section, children will be introduced to the concepts of planting and harvesting. As they engage in activities that involve planting seeds and caring for them, they will gain an appreciation of the growing things in the world around them. The weekly plan shown will assist you in creating a well-balanced literacy program. The core activities listed are designated throughout the Teacher's Guide by a blue activity square ■. Also listed are activities that take more time to complete and are especially adaptable to *full day* programs.

Throughout the Week

As you progress through your literacy program, allow time for independent reading and writing. Encourage children to engage in hands-on experiences with seeds and plants. Provide art experiences and cross-curricular activities. Set up a flower shop in the dramatic play area, sing songs, recite rhymes, and converse with children. Focus on the letters *Ll* and the letter/sound relationship.

Day 1

Reading.............**44**
Read the Story

Oral Language **45**
Respond to the Story

Writing...............**46**
Write About Work

**Full Day Extended
Time Activity** **63**
Grow Alfalfa Sprouts

Day 2

Reading...............**48**
Introduce the Letters *Ll*

Oral Language......**54**
Learn About Grains
and Breads

Writing...............**52**
Write a Chain Story

**Full Day Extended
Time Activity** **62**
Transport Seeds

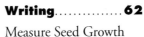

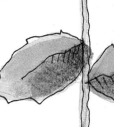

Read-Aloud Story

Theme-related literature

Read the Story

Core Activity

LITERACY OBJECTIVES

The child uses increasingly complex oral language attending to the structural elements of language appropriate for age, language background, and dialect; listens to a variety of literature to increase background information, language of books, and attention span.

MATERIALS

Story Apron, hen puppet **KIT**

Dramatize Work

• Lead children in pantomimes of work activities, such as cleaning a house or apartment and planting a garden.

• Focus on each of the steps involved in both types of work.

• Invite children to tell about times they have needed someone's help to accomplish a job or task.

Use the Story Apron

• Put on the Story Apron, indicating that it is time for a story.

• Show the hen puppet to children and ask whether they have ever seen a real hen.

The Little Red Hen

There once was a Little Red Hen who lived on a farm with a Dog, a Cat, and a Mouse. The Dog, the Cat, and the Mouse were so lazy that the Little Red Hen had to do all the work by herself.

One day the Little Red Hen found some grains of wheat.

"This wheat should be planted," she said. "Now who will help me plant the wheat?"

"Not I," said the Dog.

"Not I," said the Cat.

"Not I," said the Mouse.

"Then I'll do it myself," said the Little Red Hen. And she did.

The grains of wheat grew and grew. When it was tall and yellow, the

Little Red Hen said, "The wheat is ready to be cut. Now who will help me cut the wheat?"

"Not I," said the Dog.

"Not I," said the Cat.

"Not I," said the Mouse.

"Then I'll do it myself," said the Little Red Hen. And she did.

When the wheat was cut, the Little Red Hen said, "It's time to thresh the wheat. Now who will help me thresh the wheat?"

"Not I," said the Dog.

"Not I," said the Cat.

"Not I," said the Mouse.

"Then I'll do it myself," said the Little Red Hen. And she did.

When the wheat was threshed, the Little Red Hen put it into a sack and said, "Now who will help me take this grain to the mill and have it ground into flour?"

Introduce the Story

- Tell children that the title of the story they are going to hear is *The Little Red Hen*. Explain that the story is about a hen who grows some wheat, a plant used to make cereals and flour for bread.
- Point out that the hen in the story has a problem. As they listen to the story, invite children to make predictions about how the hen might solve her problem.

Respond to the Story

Core Activity

LITERACY OBJECTIVES
The child infers and evaluates ideas and feelings; critically analyzes information and events.

- Invite children to share the thoughts they had while you were reading the story. What did they think the Little Red Hen might do to get some help in growing the wheat? What would they have done if they were the Little Red Hen?
- Engage children in a discussion about the characters in the story. Invite them to describe the Little Red Hen and to tell how they felt about the Dog, the Cat, and the Mouse.
- Take a class vote; should the red hen have let the others share her bread or was she right not to let the other animals eat any? Encourage children to explain why they think the hen was right or wrong.

Write About Work

Core Activity

LITERACY OBJECTIVES

The child demonstrates comprehension through re-enacting stories in dramatic play and other forms; uses various forms of writing including scribble, letter-like forms, random letters/letter strings, invented spelling, and conventional spelling.

MATERIALS

Activity Sheet 5, Home-School Connection Sheet 6, paper, pencils, scissors, crayons

- Have children cut out the story characters on Activity Sheet 5 and invite them to use them to retell *The Little Red Hen* with partners. Then have children paste down the characters.
- Discuss the work the Little Red Hen does in the story. Encourage children to write about the work they do at school or at home, such as putting away toys or feeding pets. Accept all forms of writing.
- Invite children to share what they have written with the class. You may wish to keep a tally of the different types of work children do on chart paper or the chalkboard.
- Engage children in a discussion of the tasks listed. Ask them to indicate which tasks are easier when another person helps.
- Read Home-School Connection Sheet 6, which describes a baking task to be done with parents at home.

"Not I," said the Dog.

"Not I," said the Cat.

"Not I," said the Mouse.

"Then I'll do it myself," said the Little Red Hen. And she did.

When the Little Red Hen came back from the mill with the sack of flour, she said, "Now who will help me use the flour to make some bread?"

"Not I," said the Dog.

"Not I," said the Cat.

"Not I," said the Mouse.

"Then I'll do it myself," said the Little Red Hen. And she did.

The Dog, the Cat, and the Mouse sat in the doorway and watched the Little Red Hen make and bake the bread. Soon the good smell of fresh bread filled the barnyard.

Then the Little Red Hen took the bread out of the oven and said, "Now who will help me eat the bread?"

"I will!" said the Dog.

"I will!" said the Cat.

"I will!" said the Mouse.

"Oh, no you won't!" clucked the Little Red Hen. "I planted the wheat. I cut and threshed it too. I carried it to the mill, had it ground into flour, and baked the bread all by myself. Now, I will eat the bread all by myself." And she did.

Read Sentences

Core Activity

LITERACY OBJECTIVES

The child identifies some sight words; matches spoken to printed words.

MATERIALS

word card will **KIT** , *sentence strips* **KIT**

• Place the following sentence strips in a pocket chart or on a chalkboard ledge. (Create sentence strips if not available.)

"Who will help me?" said the Little Red Hen.
"Not I," said the Dog.
"Not I," said the Cat.
"Not I," said the Mouse.
"Then I'll do it myself," said the Little Red Hen. And she did.

• Invite children to identify the word *will* by matching the word card to the word in the story.

• Finger-point the sentences as you read them with children.

• Ask four children to take the parts of the Little Red Hen, the Dog, the Cat, and the Mouse and read the appropriate lines. Invite the entire class to chime in to read the final line, "And she did."

Observing the Child

When conferencing with children about their writing/drawing, invite them to read what they have written to you. As children read their writing, write their dictations on yellow sticky notes, and invite children to take them to use as models to add to their writings if they choose.

Letters and Words

Activities to increase letter knowledge

Introduce the Letters *Ll*

Core Activity

The activities suggested on this page should be used after children have learned letter names and have had multiple experiences with letters in environmental print and literature.

LITERACY OBJECTIVES
The child identifies letters of the alphabet; identifies letter/sound correspondences; uses initial letters as clues to word recognition.

MATERIALS
classroom alphabet picture cards **KIT** *, picture cards* **KIT** *, lap-sized chalkboards* **KIT** *, manipulative letters* **KIT** *, or available alphabet picture cards and manipulative letters (Adapt activity for use with your materials.)*

Recognize the Letter
- Write the word *leaf* on the chalkboard and tell children that the word *leaf* begins with the letter *l*.
- Circle or underline the letter.
- Point to and name the letters *Ll* on the classroom alphabet picture card.
- Write the letters on the chalkboard, inviting children to trace the letters in the air with their fingers.
- Encourage small groups of children to write the letters on lap-sized chalkboards.
- Have children identify *Ll* manipulative letters and use them as models for their own writing.
- Invite children to make the letter *L* by gluing shoelaces on felt or cardboard. Alternatively, invite children to practice writing the letters on paper.

Hear the Sound for the Letter

- Point to and identify the key word picture of a leaf on the classroom alphabet picture card.
- Say the word *leaf* for children, emphasizing the l sound at the beginning of the word.
- As children say the word with you, draw attention to how the sound is formed in the mouth.
- Have children listen as you say the following words. Ask them to nod their heads when the word begins with the same sound they hear at the beginning of the word *leaf*.

| list | hammer | face | laugh | lady |
| yell | leap | watch | loud | line |

- Have children identify the picture cards that begin with the l sound—lamp, lettuce, and lion.
- Invite children to name things they might see when taking a nature walk, such as a *log, lake, land,* and *lawn*.

Relate the Letter with the Sound

- Brainstorm with children a list of things that grow from seeds and write the words on the chalkboard. Circle words beginning with *l*. Possible words include *lettuce, lima bean, lawn, lime, lemon, leaves,* and *leek*. Children might enjoy creating a book of these words, illustrating and labeling each word beginning with *l*.
- Have children write sentences using the following patterns:

    I like _____.
    I love _____!

Invite children to use invented spelling. Bind children's writing into a booklet, read it aloud, then place it in the Literacy Center for additional readings.

Just for Fun

Let's Make Celery Cars

Ingredients
celery, carrots, peanut butter, raisins

Cut celery into 2-inch pieces and cut carrot circles. Have children fill the centers of celery with peanut butter. Dab peanut butter in the center of the carrot circles and place on each side of celery to make wheels. Children can decorate their cars with raisins if they choose.

Kindergarteners Read

Activities that foster reading development

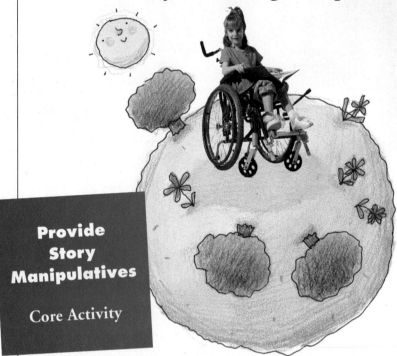

Provide Story Manipulatives

Core Activity

LITERACY OBJECTIVES

The child selects materials and participates in voluntary and/or independent reading; retells stories demonstrating a sense of story structure including an understanding of setting, theme, plot episodes, and resolution.

MATERIALS

books, hen puppet **KIT** *, story sequence cards* **KIT** *, audiocassette tape* Kindergarten Ecology—side 2 **KIT** *, writing/drawing materials*

Show children the new materials available in the library corner that relate to the theme *Growing Things* or to the read-aloud story, such as picture books, *The Little Red Hen* story sequence cards, the hen puppet, and the audiocassette tape. Invite children to choose among the following independent reading and story retelling activities.

- Listen to the audiocassette tape of *The Little Red Hen* and draw pictures showing their favorite parts of the story.
- Use *The Little Red Hen* story sequence cards to retell the story to a partner or classroom visitor.
- Alone or with a partner, draw or rewrite a new version of *The Little Red Hen* in which the Dog, Cat, and Mouse help with the work.

Observing the Child

The ability to predict is an indicator of how successful one will be both in reading and in understanding what is being read. Children who have had books read to them and who have had varied background experiences are more likely to be able to predict what a poem or a story is going to be about. Note which children are able to make predictions based on the title and illustrations. Throughout the year, be aware of the progress individual children make in predicting.

Read *Little Celebrations* Book

Core Activity

LITERACY OBJECTIVES

The child makes progress in moving toward conventional reading of print; participates in collaborative reading activities.

MATERIALS

Potatoes on Tuesday *by Dee Lillegard*

For Shared Reading

• Introduce the book, reading the title and by-lines, and encouraging children to examine the cover illustration to predict what they think this book might be about. Invite children to share their favorite ways to eat potatoes.

• Read the book aloud, pausing for children's comments about the illustrations.

• You might use the illustrations to help children discover the different ways that vegetables grow—under the ground, above the ground, on a plant, in a pod, and on a vine.

• Reread the book, helping children discover that they can use the pattern of progressing weekdays and the illustrations to read along with you.

For Emergent Reading

• Encourage children to identify the days of the week named in the book and to find the names on the classroom calendar.

Respond to the Book

• Invite children to work alone or in pairs to make vegetable books illustrating which vegetables are their favorites to eat.

Sequence Steps in a Process

Optional Activity

LITERACY OBJECTIVES

The child follows oral directions; critically analyzes information and events.

MATERIALS

vinyl storyboard and manipulatives Steps in a Process **KIT** , *word cards* tree, flower, plant, fruit, *and* vegetable **KIT**

• Encourage children to review the sequence of steps that the Little Red Hen went through as she made the bread. Suggest to children that many things in nature happen in a certain order.

• Pairs of children can work together to sequence the five sets of *Steps in a Process* vinyl manipulatives, placing them in the order in which they happen from left to right.

• As children are working, encourage them to discuss with each other why the steps occur in a specific order.

• Introduce the word cards and invite children to match them to the vinyl storyboard and manipulatives, identifying the flower, vegetable, or plants shown.

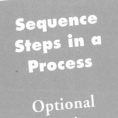

Kindergarteners Write

Activities that foster writing development

Write a Chain Story

Core Activity

LITERACY OBJECTIVES

The child uses literature as a model for writing; attends to and contributes to a print-rich environment by making books and writing stories.

MATERIALS

chart paper, marker, a variety of plants, including a bean plant

- Invite children to listen as you read or tell the story of *Jack and the Beanstalk*.
- Discuss the growth of the plant in the story.
- Tell children they will be writing another story about a plant that grows.

- You may wish to start the story by writing "Once upon a time . . ." on chart paper. Invite each child to add a sentence to the story as you record it on the chart paper. Point out that the plant in the story may grow any way children choose and that they may include as many characters as they wish.
- Read the completed story to children.

Record Birdfeeder Activity

Core Activity

LITERACY OBJECTIVES

The child uses various forms of writing; writes in a variety of genres.

MATERIALS

empty milk cartons, twigs, birdseed, string, scissors, writing materials

- List on the chalkboard children's suggestions about foods they would place in a birdfeeder, pointing out that some birds enjoy eating seeds.
- Invite children, working in groups, to construct their own birdfeeders. Help children cut the top off a milk carton, and then poke a stick through both sides of the carton. Next, have children attach a string to each end of the stick and fill the bottom of the carton with birdseed.
- Let each group select a place to hang their birdfeeder and help them attach it securely.
- Encourage children to check their birdfeeders daily and to keep records of their observations by writing descriptions of the birds that visit.

Create Seed Packets

Core Activity

LITERACY OBJECTIVES

The child participates in collaborative writing activities; makes progress toward writing readable text.

MATERIALS

a variety of fruits seeds, plastic bags, writing/drawing materials

- Talk with children about how most flowers, fruits, and plants grow from seeds. Read or display books such as *A Flower Grows* by Ken Robbins (Dial Books, 1990) and *The Empty Pot* by Demi (Holt, 1990).
- Display a variety of fruit seeds, such as orange, apple, and watermelon seeds, and peach, cherry, and plum pits.
- Encourage children to identify the fruit that grows from each seed as you list the names on the chalkboard.
- Ask children to select two or three different types of seeds and sort them into plastic bags. Have them label the bags with the name of each fruit, using the list on the chalkboard as a model.
- Invite children to create seed packets for their seeds by drawing pictures of what the seeds will look like when they are full-grown and inserting them into the appropriate bags.
- Collect all the seed packets and display them in an area where children can examine them.
- After a week you may wish to invite children to bring their seeds home to plant.

Oral Language

Activities focusing on speaking and listening

Learn About Grains and Bread

Core Activity

Talk About Planting

Core Activity

LITERACY OBJECTIVES

The child makes use of an environment rich in literacy materials; engages freely in conversation in varied situations.

LITERACY OBJECTIVES

The child uses increased vocabulary throughout the year; makes use of an environment rich in literacy materials.

MATERIALS

picture books, grain seeds, bread or crackers

- Invite children to recall how the Little Red Hen planted and grew wheat, then baked the wheat into bread.
- Read books such as *From Grain to Bread* by Ali Mitgutsch (Carolrhoda, 1981) or *Bread, Bread, Bread* by Ann Morris (Lothrop, Lee, & Shepard, 1989). Discuss with children the types of grain grown for use in breads and crackers.
- Bring in a variety of grain seeds, such as corn, wheat, rice, and oats. Invite children to compare the way the different seeds look, smell, and feel.
- If feasible, provide bread or crackers made from each type of grain and encourage children to sample them. Invite children to describe and contrast the different textures and flavors.

- Use the story of *The Little Red Hen* to launch a discussion about planting, growing, and harvesting. Read books such as Jill Krementz's *A Very Young Gardener* to provide further background.
- Encourage children to imagine that they are planting their own gardens. What fruits, vegetables, or flowers would they like to grow?
- Invite children to pantomime planting activities, beginning with digging holes to plant seeds, watering and weeding, and finally picking the fruits, vegetables, or flowers.
- Write the words *Spring, Summer, Fall,* and *Winter* on the chalkboard. Invite children to provide words that describe the planting activity for each season.

Make Alphabet Books

Core Activity

LITERACY OBJECTIVES

The child pronounces speech sounds and words appropriately for age, language background, and dialect; identifies letters of the alphabet; uses phonics and picture clues to help identify words.

MATERIALS

Activity Sheets 7-12, writing materials

The Alphabet Book (Activity Sheets 7-12) provides opportunities for children to explore concepts about things that grow, the weather, the calendar, and seasons of the year, as well as enhancing letter recognition and writing skills. Because of the multiple learning opportunities on these pages, the Alphabet Book is ideally suited to week-long use.

• Call children's attention to the calendar on each page and read the names of the months. Encourage children to relate the months to the seasonal scenes shown.

• Invite children to examine each picture, identifying plants and discussing the time of year shown. Have children describe what they see in the scenes.

• Help children read the word labels for the objects on each page, calling their attention to the initial letters.

• Encourage children to practice writing letters of the alphabet in the boxes provided.

Dramatic Play

Implementing dramatic play centers

**Visit the
Flower Shop**

Extended Time
Activity

FLOWER SHOP EQUIPMENT AND MATERIALS

*shelves for display
cash register
telephone
plants
pots for planting
soil
seeds
trowel
watering can*

LITERACY MATERIALS

*telephone book
seed and bulb catalogs
flower seed packets
plant care and
    gardening books
brochures from florists
greeting cards
paper, pencils
flower charts
flower shop posters
construction paper
Blackline Master 2*

Visit a local flower shop, the floral department in a grocery store, or walk around the neighborhood to see where flowers have been planted. Note the varieties and colors of flowers. Discuss with children why people like to have flowers in their homes and in their gardens, and talk about occasions when people send flowers to one another. If possible, have a floral worker demonstrate how a floral display is made and tell how the flowers are shipped from other countries such as Mexico to flower markets in the United States.

- Provide seed and bulb catalogs, flower seed packets, and flower books for children to look at.
- Encourage children to plant seeds in individual containers, to care for the plants, and to log the plants' growth in observation journals.
- Place home gardening and plant care books in the center.
- Invite children to make a flower collage using catalog pictures.
- Provide brochures showing floral bouquets and arrangements that are available at local florist shops.
- Encourage children to do a survey of favorite colors of flowers and then make charts recording those colors.

- After looking at catalogs, have children list the names of favorite flowers on a chart and illustrate them. Display the chart in the shop so that customers can refer to the chart when ordering.
- Have children brainstorm materials they can use to make flowers, such as gluing tissue paper on construction paper. Demonstrate how to make petals curl by wrapping them around a pencil.
- Invite children to paint large flowers at the easels.
- Demonstrate how orders for flowers are taken on the telephone by modeling conversation regarding the cost of bouquets, color and flower choices, and where to send the arrangements or plants.
- Show samples of greeting cards that are attached to bouquets and then have children make their own.
- Provide Blackline Master 2, Customer Order Blank and Greeting Cards.

Art

Creative extensions of the section topic

**Make a
Seed Mosaic**

Optional
Activity

LITERACY OBJECTIVE

The child follows oral directions.

MATERIALS

large plastic lids, glue, assorted seeds, string

- Fill shallow trays or dishes with dry seeds, such as beans, peas, watermelon, sunflower, and corn seeds. Label each tray with a picture or word to help children identify the seed types.
- Have children spread a layer of glue inside the tops of plastic lids. Invite children to place different types of seeds on the glue to create a mosaic design.
- Before the glue dries completely, have children peel the mosaic from the lid.
- Poke a hole in each mosaic, insert a string through it, and allow it to dry completely.
- When the mosaics are completed, they can be hung in a window for the class to enjoy.

Design a Potato Head

Extended Time Activity

LITERACY OBJECTIVE
The child engages freely in conversation in varied situations.

MATERIALS
large potatoes, grass seed, spoons, cotton, art materials, water

- Lead children in a discussion about how seeds grow, including how a seed is planted and tended as it grows.
- Help children scoop a hole out of the top of a potato and fill it with moist cotton.
- Provide art supplies such as buttons, beads, sequins, corks, toothpicks, and yarn, and invite children to attach them to the potatoes to create funny faces.
- Have children sprinkle grass seed on the cotton in the tops of their potatoes.
- Help children care for their potato heads by placing them upright near a window, and keeping the cotton moist.
- In a few days grass will appear and children may wish to give their potato heads "haircuts."
- Grass hair can also be grown in a paper or plastic cup filled with soil.

Music

Songs and activities related to the section topic

Play a Circle Game

Optional Activity

LITERACY OBJECTIVES
The child attends to adult models of writing; matches spoken to printed words.

MATERIALS
watering can, yellow construction paper

Fine Arts

"Oats, Peas, Beans and Barley Grow"

- Write the words to the song on the chalkboard. Finger-point the words as the song is spoken as a chant.
- Choose a child to hold a watering can and another to hold a paper sun. Invite the rest of class to form a circle, crouching down to represent seeds.
- As the song is sung, the child with the watering can and the sun "water" and "shine" on the seeds. As the water and sun move around the circle, the children in the circle slowly begin to rise.
- Repeat the song and activity, inviting two new children to hold the sun and the watering can.
- Encourage children to name other types of seeds that grow and then sing the song using the new words.

Make a Seed Shaker

Extended Time Activity

LITERACY OBJECTIVES
The child follows oral directions; knows that words are made up of syllables.

MATERIALS
audiocassette tape Kindergarten Ecology— *side 2* **KIT** *, plastic, metal, or glass containers with lids; dry seeds such as oats, peas, beans, and barley*

- Display dry seeds and help children identify them.
- Encourage children to name things the seeds would require in order to grow, such as water, light, and soil.
- Provide a container for each child. Ask children to choose one type of seed, add a handful of those seeds to the containers, and cover with lids.
- Invite children to use their containers to shake the beats or syllables of the words as they listen to the song on the audiocassette tape.
- Have children form small groups, choosing one child to be the conductor. As the music plays, invite the conductor to point to each group, indicating when they should join in with their seed shakers.

Oats, Peas, Beans and Barley Grow

Oats, peas, beans and bar - ley grow,

Oats, peas, beans and bar - ley grow. Can you or I or

an - y - one know How oats, peas, beans and bar - ley grow?

Across the Curriculum

Math, science, social studies, health activities

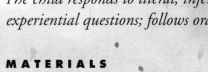

Measure Seed Growth

Core Activity

LITERACY OBJECTIVE
The child writes for a variety of purposes.

MATERIALS
baby food jars or plastic cups, soil, lima beans, water, posterboard, tape, writing materials

Mathematics

- Engage children in a discussion about how plants grow and what they need to grow.
- Invite children to write their names on pieces of tape and attach the name tags to jars or cups.
- Have children fill each container half full of soil, plant a lima bean, and care for the plants by making sure they have water each day. Place the seed plants in a sunny area.
- Provide each child with a strip of posterboard or cardboard. Encourage children to observe and measure the growth of plants by marking the height from soil to tip of the plants on the strips. Children can compare the marks to see how much the plants grow over the course of a week.

Transport Seeds

Extended Time Activity

LITERACY OBJECTIVES
The child responds to literal, inferential, and experiential questions; follows oral directions.

MATERIALS
a pair of old white socks for each child, large trays filled with soil, strips of posterboard or cardboard

Science

- Invite children to name things that grow in a variety of places. Talk about how plant seeds are spread from one place to another when they are carried on the wind, or on insects, people, and animals.
- Have children put on old pairs of socks over their shoes and go on a walk around the neighborhood.
- Occasionally have children examine their socks and describe what they find on them. Point out that this is one way people transport seeds from one place to another.
- Invite children to shake their socks over a tray of soil in the classroom. Place the tray in a sunny spot.
- Invite children to water the soil daily and watch for shoots that may begin to appear. Encourage children to try to identify plants that sprout in the soil.

Grow Alfalfa Sprouts

Extended Time Activity

LITERACY OBJECTIVES

The child engages freely in conversation in varied situations; attends to adult models of literacy behaviors.

MATERIALS

alfalfa seeds, baby food jars, cheesecloth, rubber bands, water, index cards, tape

Health

- Reread Rhyme Poster 12, "Sprouts!". Tell children that they are going to grow alfalfa sprouts.
- Invite groups of children to fill jars half full of water, add two tablespoons of seeds to the water, and soak overnight.
- The next day, drain the water, cover the jar openings with cheesecloth, secure with a rubber band, and lay the jars on their sides in a dark place.
- Have children rinse the sprouts two times a day by filling the jars with water and draining the excess water. After each rinsing return the jars to a dark place.
- On the fourth day, invite children to place their sprouts by a sunny window and have them observe how the sun turns sprouts green.
- Encourage children to taste their sprouts. Use the sprouts and other ingredients to make a healthy salad for the class.

Observe How Plants "Drink Water"

Optional Activity

LITERACY OBJECTIVES

The child takes turns appropriately when engaged in conversation; responds to literal, inferential, and experiential questions.

MATERIALS

celery, red food coloring, glasses

Science

- Invite children to tell stories about activities that make them thirsty.
- Ask children to name things they drink to quench their thirst as you list them on the chalkboard.
- Have pairs of children place a stalk of celery in a glass of colored water for several hours, checking it frequently to observe any changes.
- After a few hours, children should observe that the celery changes color from bottom to top.
- Encourage children to discuss the changes they see. Lead children to understand that the celery "drank" water from the jar, just as plants "drink" water from the ground or soil.

Books to Enjoy

Books related to the section topic

Ardley, Neil. *The Science of Things That Grow*. New York: Harcourt Brace Jovanovich, 1991. Simple experiments help children learn basic principles and interesting facts about growing things.

Arnold, Caroline. *Sun Fun*. New York: Franklin Watts, 1981. This book is filled with sun-related experiments that young readers can do.

Arnosky, Jim. *Raccoons and Ripe Corn*. New York: Lothrop, 1987. The artist's lifelike illustrations tell a story of raccoons who live near a farm.

Demi. *The Empty Pot*. New York: Holt, 1990. The child who raises the best flower from a seed will become the new Emperor. The children do not know that the seeds they have been given are cooked ones.

Dineen, Jacqueline. *Let's Look at Rain*. New York: Bookwright Press, 1989. Children will learn that rain is crucial to growing things.

Ehlert, Lois. *Growing Vegetable Soup*. San Diego: Harcourt, 1987. Bright colors and bold graphics make this a vegetable garden to remember.

Krementz, Jill. *A Very Young Gardener*. New York: Dial Books, 1991. A six-year-old learns about conservation as she plants and tends her own garden.

McMillan, Bruce. *Counting Wildflowers*. New York: Lothrop, 1986. The concepts of counting, colors, and flowers are reinforced by vibrant photographs.

_____. *Growing Colors*. New York: Lothrop, 1988.Viewers will enjoy identifying colors as they look at photographs of fruits and vegetables.

Mitgutsch, Ali. *From Grain to Bread*. Minneapolis: Carolrhoda Books, 1981. Children learn how grain is planted, grown, harvested, and finally baked into bread.

Morris, Ann. *Bread, Bread, Bread*. Photographs by Ken Heyman. New York: Lothrop, 1989. Enticing photos introduce readers to breads from around the world, including French baguettes, tortillas, pita bread, and pretzels.

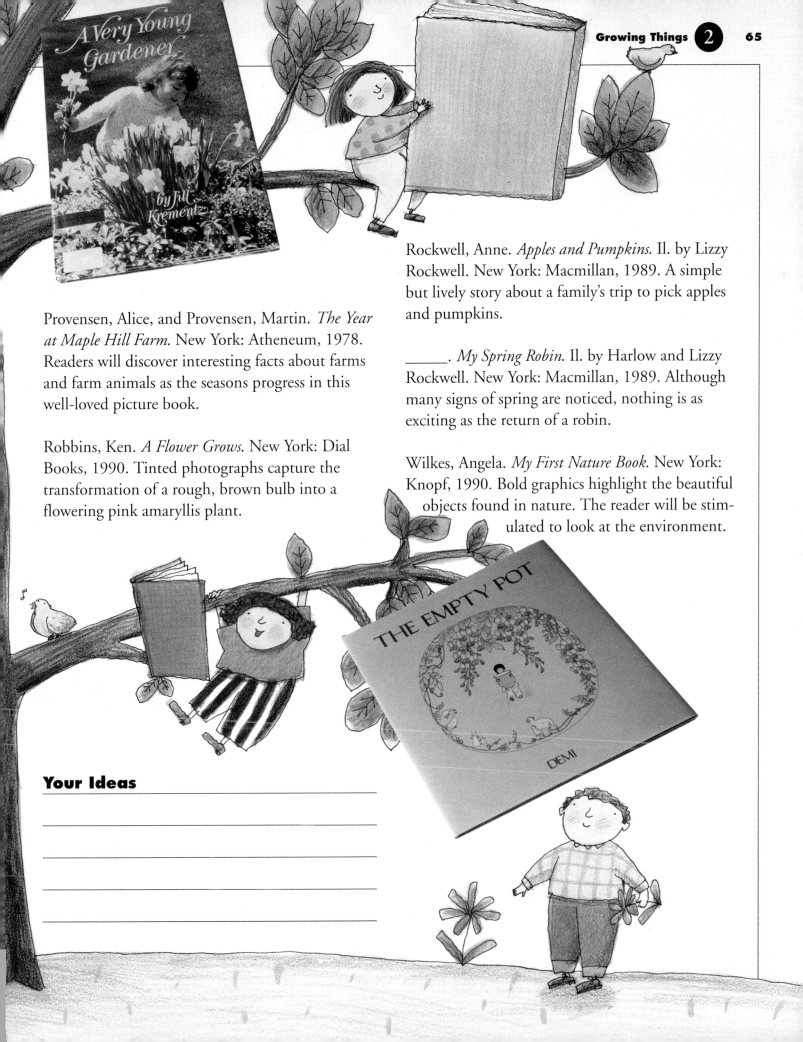

Provensen, Alice, and Provensen, Martin. *The Year at Maple Hill Farm.* New York: Atheneum, 1978. Readers will discover interesting facts about farms and farm animals as the seasons progress in this well-loved picture book.

Robbins, Ken. *A Flower Grows.* New York: Dial Books, 1990. Tinted photographs capture the transformation of a rough, brown bulb into a flowering pink amaryllis plant.

Rockwell, Anne. *Apples and Pumpkins.* Il. by Lizzy Rockwell. New York: Macmillan, 1989. A simple but lively story about a family's trip to pick apples and pumpkins.

_____. *My Spring Robin.* Il. by Harlow and Lizzy Rockwell. New York: Macmillan, 1989. Although many signs of spring are noticed, nothing is as exciting as the return of a robin.

Wilkes, Angela. *My First Nature Book.* New York: Knopf, 1990. Bold graphics highlight the beautiful objects found in nature. The reader will be stimulated to look at the environment.

Your Ideas
_____
_____
_____
_____
_____

Section ③

Earth Day

Background Information

Today's children are inheriting an environment in need of restoration, purification, and balance. In this section, children become more aware of environmental concerns and learn how to be responsible to the world in their daily lives.

Air pollution from vehicle exhaust and industry affects plants, animals, people, and bodies of water. The burning of fossil fuels (coal and oil) releases gases that mix with moisture in the air to form *acid rain* containing sulfuric and nitric acids. Acid rain is harmful to trees and plants and upsets the chemical balance of lakes, ponds, and streams.

Deforestation occurs mostly in parts of Central and South America, Africa, and Asia. As trees are cleared from these areas to provide land for farming, animals lose their habitat, the soil is eroded, and less oxygen is generated into the air because there are fewer plants and trees.

Water pollution from litter, chemicals dumped from factories, and oil dumped from industry or tankers affects wildlife, transportation, and recreational land.

The layer of *ozone*, a type of gas that protects the earth's surface from ultraviolet radiation from the sun, is being depleted by chlorofluorocarbons (CFCs) released into the air from aerosol sprays, plastic foam, and refrigeration. Skin conditions in humans, plus damage to plants and animals can result from too much ultraviolet exposure.

Landfills, areas where garbage is taken, are overflowing as less land is available because of development. Recycling can help reduce the amount of material in landfills, but not all waste can be recycled.

Every Day

The following are possible classroom activities for this section.

- Engage children in a schoolyard or community cleanup.
- Visit a recycling center.
- Donate old toys, outgrown clothing, and other unwanted items to charitable organizations.
- Set up a classroom recycling center.
- Visit a grocery story to examine the packaging of products on the shelves. Identify recyclable plastics, glass, aluminum, and cardboard. Watch for overpackaging or non-recyclable items.
- Write letters to conservation and wildlife organizations and environmental groups. Learn about programs currently underway to help the environment.

Core Literacy Activities

A core activity plan for the week

Getting Started

Children today are more aware of the environment, and the importance of maintaining its balance, than ever before. Section 3, *Earth Day Every Day*, invites children to express their appreciation for our planet and to take steps toward insuring its health and preserving its beauty. The weekly plan shown will assist you in creating a well-balanced literacy program. The core activities listed are designated throughout the Teacher's Guide by a blue activity square ■. Also listed are activities that take more time to complete and are especially adaptable to *full day* programs.

Throughout the Week

As you progress through your literacy program, allow time for independent reading and writing; also provide art experiences and cross-curricular activities. Set up a camping area in the dramatic play area, sing songs, recite rhymes and fingerplays, and converse with children.

Celebrating What We've Learned

During the fourth week of the unit, have kindergarteners "Lead the Way to Earth Day" as they participate in the culminating project. Reread books and rhyme posters, and encourage reading and writing activities.

Spring Rain
by Marchette Chute

The storm came up so very quick
It couldn't have been quicker.
I should have brought my hat along,
I should have brought my slicker.

My hair is wet, my feet are wet,
I couldn't be much wetter.
I fell into a river once
But this is even better.

I'm Glad the Sky Is Painted Blue
Anonymous

I'm glad the sky is painted blue,
And the earth is painted green,
With such a lot of nice fresh air
All sandwiched in between.

Berry Picking
by Bobbi Katz

Strawberries,
        strawberries—
yum, yum, yummy!
One for the pail
        and
two for the tummy!

One to save
        and
two to taste—
lots to pick
        and
none to waste!

Anti-Pollution Rap
by Sonja Dunn

Don't throw your garbage
Out on the street
Keep your planet
Clean and neat
Put your wrappers
In the big round bin
Recycle cans
That are made of tin
Take your bottles
Back to the store
Get a refund
To buy some more
Never toss junk
From a moving auto
'Cause "Clean is keen"
Should be your motto

Rhyme Posters

Theme-related literature

Use Rhyme Poster 25

Core Activity

LITERACY OBJECTIVES

The child enjoys the rhyme and rhythm of poetry; pronounces speech sounds and words appropriately for age, language background, and dialect.

MATERIALS

rhyme poster 25 "Spring Rain," audiocassette tape Kindergarten Ecology—side 1 **KIT** *, picture books*

• Read the poem aloud and invite children to tell how they feel about rain and storms. Ask them to tell whether they enjoy getting wet in the rain.

• Invite children to think of words that describe how rain sounds and feels, and how things look when they are wet with rain. Record the words on the chalkboard and use them to generate a class poem about rain.

• Provide nonfictional books about weather for children to look at and read.

• Discuss appropriate dress for varying weather conditions. Provide a raincoat, rain hat, boots, and an umbrella for children to wear in dramatic play.

• Talk about how rainfall and water help plants, animals, and people.

Spring Rain
by Marchette Chute

The storm came up so very quick
    It couldn't have been quicker.
I should have brought my hat along,
    I should have brought my slicker.

My hair is wet, my feet are wet,
    I couldn't be much wetter.
I fell into a river once
    But this is even better.

Rhyme Poster #25/Kindergarten Ecology

Use Rhyme Poster 26

Core Activity

LITERACY OBJECTIVES

The child enjoys the rhyme and rhythm of poetry; uses various forms of writing.

MATERIALS

rhyme poster 26 "I'm Glad the Sky Is Painted Blue," audiocassette tape Kindergarten Ecology—side 1 **KIT**

- Read the poem aloud. Invite children to name other colors seen in nature, such as the yellow sun, an orange sunset, a red rose, or green grass and to tell which colors they like best.
- Set up a nature display in the classroom. Invite children to bring in natural items such as pine cones, rocks, twigs, and leaves. Discuss how each item is helpful to people and animals.
- Some people are fond of being in or around water, while others like to dig and plant in the earth. Some people enjoy studying trees and others like to collect rocks. What natural things do children like? Ask them to write or draw their preferences.
- Listen to each poem in the unit on the audiocassette tape. Encourage children to dramatize the poems.

I'm Glad the Sky Is Painted Blue

Anonymous

I'm glad the sky is painted blue,
  And the earth is painted green,
With such a lot of nice fresh air
  All sandwiched in between.

Rhyme Poster #26/Kindergarten Ecology

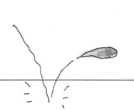

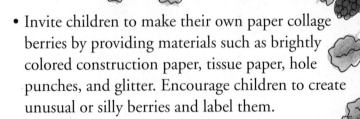

**Use Rhyme
Poster 27**

Core Activity

LITERACY OBJECTIVES

The child enjoys the rhyme and rhythm of poetry; makes use of an environment rich in literacy materials.

MATERIALS

rhyme poster 27 "Berry Picking," audiocassette tape Kindergarten Ecology—side 1 **KIT** , *picture books by Lois Ehlert, art materials*

Fine Arts

- Read the poem to children. Lead children on a pantomime through a berry patch or garden. Recite the poem as you fill your pails with strawberries.
- Invite children to name berries they have tasted. Encourage them to think of the many things made from berries, such as pies, juices, jellies, jams, and yogurt.
- If feasible, bring juices or yogurt into class and have a tasting party. Encourage children to note differences in color and taste.
- Invite children to compare the art on rhyme poster 27 with the art in *Little Celebrations* Book *Big Pig, Little Pig* and other books by Lois Ehlert, such as *Color Farm* (Lippincott, 1990) and *Feathers for Lunch* (Harcourt, 1990). Note similarities in color, style, and texture.
- Explain that the illustrator has created beautiful art forms from paper cutouts.

Berry Picking
by Bobbi Katz

Strawberries,
    strawberries—
yum, yum, yummy!
One for the pail
    and
two for the tummy!

One to save
    and
two to taste—
lots to pick
    and
none to waste!

- Invite children to make their own paper collage berries by providing materials such as brightly colored construction paper, tissue paper, hole punches, and glitter. Encourage children to create unusual or silly berries and label them.

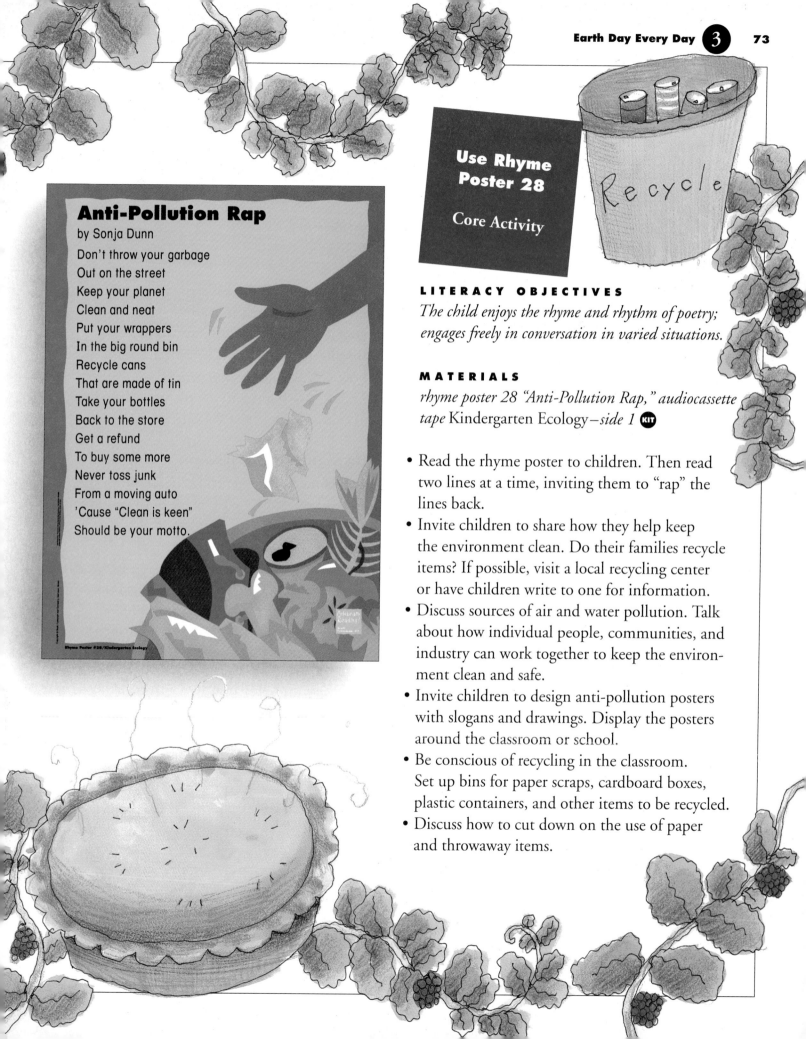

Anti-Pollution Rap
by Sonja Dunn

Don't throw your garbage
Out on the street
Keep your planet
Clean and neat
Put your wrappers
In the big round bin
Recycle cans
That are made of tin
Take your bottles
Back to the store
Get a refund
To buy some more
Never toss junk
From a moving auto
'Cause "Clean is keen"
Should be your motto.

Rhyme Poster #28/Kindergarten Ecology

Use Rhyme Poster 28

Core Activity

LITERACY OBJECTIVES
The child enjoys the rhyme and rhythm of poetry; engages freely in conversation in varied situations.

MATERIALS
rhyme poster 28 "Anti-Pollution Rap," audiocassette tape Kindergarten Ecology—side 1 **KIT**

- Read the rhyme poster to children. Then read two lines at a time, inviting them to "rap" the lines back.
- Invite children to share how they help keep the environment clean. Do their families recycle items? If possible, visit a local recycling center or have children write to one for information.
- Discuss sources of air and water pollution. Talk about how individual people, communities, and industry can work together to keep the environment clean and safe.
- Invite children to design anti-pollution posters with slogans and drawings. Display the posters around the classroom or school.
- Be conscious of recycling in the classroom. Set up bins for paper scraps, cardboard boxes, plastic containers, and other items to be recycled.
- Discuss how to cut down on the use of paper and throwaway items.

Kindergarteners Read

Activities that foster reading development

Read *Little* Celebrations Book

Core Activity

LITERACY OBJECTIVES

The child enjoys the rhythm and rhyme of poetry and other literature genres; makes progress in moving toward conventional reading of print; uses syntax, context, phonics clues, picture clues, and memory to help identify words.

MATERIALS

Recycling Dump *by Andrea Butler*

For Shared Reading

- Invite children to look at the cover illustration as you read the title and by-lines. You may want to discuss the word *recycle* before reading.
- What things do children predict they might see being recycled in this book?
- Read the book aloud, inviting children to join in on the repetitive sound words.
- Reread the book, helping children discover that they can use the repetition and picture clues to read along with you.

For Emergent Reading

- Encourage children to read the books with a partner and point out words they know. Can they tell their partners how they recognize these words?
- Encourage children to use picture clues as they read.

Respond to the Book

- Did children enjoy reading the sound words in this book? You might point out that authors sometimes use sound words to make their books exciting to listen to and read.
- If your school or community does not already recycle, encourage children to brainstorm things they could bring in to begin recycling.
- Have small groups of children think about materials they could bring from home, such as yarn, foam pieces, or buttons to be recycled and incorporated into children's art work.
- Encourage children to bring from home greeting cards that can be recycled at the writing table or in the art center.

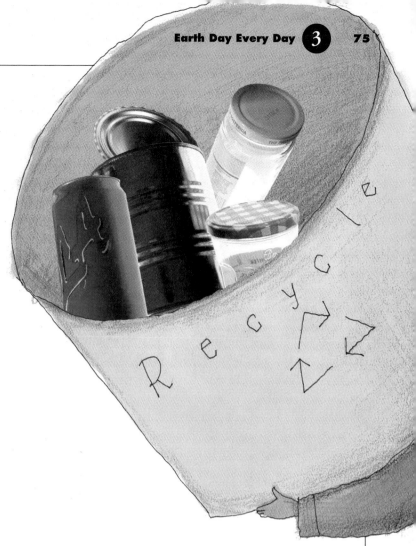

Read Environmental Print

Optional Activity

LITERACY OBJECTIVES

The child recognizes environmental print; attends to and contributes to a print-rich environment by making books and writing stories.

MATERIALS

various types of environmental print including cans, bottles, newspapers, and cereal boxes; writing/drawing materials

- Children may be surprised at the words they are able to read independently.
- Provide children with various types of environmental print. You might use cans, bottles, and newspapers that you are collecting to recycle.
- Encourage children to discover how many different environmental words they are able to read on their own.
- Invite children to point out and read some of the words they know to friends, small groups, or the class.
- They might want to copy and illustrate their words into books titled *Look What I Can Read!*
- Encourage children to bring from home food labels from cans and boxes, advertisements, and flyers, and then create class alphabet books using the labels. Children will enjoy reading the names of the products again and again.

Just for Fun

Recycle to Make Rainbow Crayons

Recycle broken or small crayons to make rainbow crayons for drawing. Have children peel off remaining paper from crayons, break crayons into small pieces, and place into muffin tins. Heat in oven until wax is melted; then remove and let stand until cool (do not stir or colors will become muddy looking). Once crayons have hardened, remove from tins.

Kindergarteners Write

Activities that foster writing development

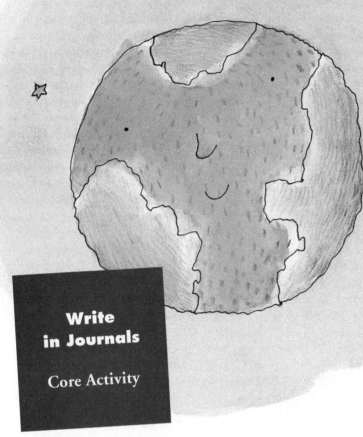

Collect Litter

Core Activity

LITERACY OBJECTIVE
The child attends to adult models of writing.

MATERIALS
"litter," nature objects, paperbags, writing materials, tongs or small plastic bags

- Display several kinds of litter such as a gum wrapper, a piece of paper, or an empty soda can along with several nature objects such as a pine cone, a twig, and a leaf.
- Explain to children that litter is garbage which has not been disposed of properly. Invite children to identify the items that are litter and throw them into a garbage can.
- Encourage children to write *litterbag* on paperbags.
- Discuss with children what kinds of litter are appropriate to include in a cleanup and then have children search the playground for litter and collect it in their bags. Have children use tongs, or plastic bags to cover their hands as they pick up litter.
- Ask children to discard the litter in a large garbage can or bin and note the total amount collected. Discuss what the world would look like if no one collected litter.

Write in Journals

Core Activity

LITERACY OBJECTIVES
The child makes progress toward writing readable text; selects writing materials and chooses to write independently.

MATERIALS
journals, pencils

Encourage children to write descriptions or stories about what they can do to help make the earth a good place to live.

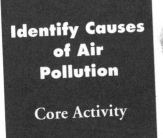

**Identify Causes
of Air
Pollution**

Core Activity

LITERACY OBJECTIVES

*The child understands the correspondence between
spoken and written words in dictation when used;
attends to adult models of writing.*

MATERIALS

flashlight, tape recorder, chart paper

- Encourage children to look around the
  room and ask them if they think any noticeable
  particles are in the air.
- Have a child turn off the lights and shine a
  flashlight in front of children. Then ask children
  to describe the particles they see in the air.
- Guide a discussion in which children become
  aware that when there are too many particles
  present in the air it is called air pollution.
- Invite children to take a walk around the
  neighborhood to "hunt" for things that cause air
  pollution, such as exhaust from trucks and cars,
  factories, and construction machinery. Each time
  they spot something that causes air pollution,
  have a child identify the name of the object on
  the tape recorder.
- After returning to the classroom, play the tape
  to help make a list of things in the neighborhood
  that might contribute to air pollution.

Observing the Child

When conferencing with
children about their writing/
drawing,
- invite them to tell you about
  what they have written.
- ask them if they would like to
  add to it or write more about it.
- ask them what they think they
  will write/draw about next.

- Have children watch as you list the names on
  chart paper. Invite children to help you sound
  out and spell some of the words as you write.
  Car. *What sound do you hear at the beginning of
  the word* car? *The c sound. Right. Now, I know the
  next letter in the word is an* a. *What sound do you
  hear next? You hear the r sound so the letter is* r.
- Have children brainstorm possible solutions to
  the air pollution problems in the neighborhood,
  accepting all reasonable answers.

Oral Language

Activities focusing on speaking and listening

LITERACY OBJECTIVES
The child attends to adult models of rich oral language; uses increased vocabulary throughout the year.

MATERIALS
Activity Sheets 13-14, scissors, crayons, stapler

- Involve children in a discussion of what they would need to take on a camping trip. List items on a chart.
- Talk about what is involved in each of these camping tasks:

  getting water, finding wood for the fire, cooking, setting up the tents (or space for sleeping bags)

- Involve children in a discussion about responsibility to the environment when camping. Discuss picking up litter, leaving the campsite the way it was found, and the importance of making sure campfires are out.
- Demonstrate how to cut out the camper and sleeping bag on Activity Sheets 13-14.
- After children have folded the bags, help them staple the sides. Invite children to use the cut-out campers and sleeping bags to make up camping stories or for acting out camping scenes.

Observing the Child

To stimulate thinking, problem solving, and to develop oral language skills, give children frequent opportunities to answer literal, inferential, and experiential questions. Determine which children are able to listen when questions are being asked and then which children are able to respond reasonably. Give children opportunities to explain their responses to questions and to be courteous listeners when other children speak. Some children have had limited opportunities to speak to and to be heard by adults.

Share a Poem

Core Activity

LITERACY OBJECTIVES

The child enjoys the rhythm and rhyme of poetry; uses increasingly complex oral language.

Happy Thought

*The world is so full
of a number of things,
I'm sure we should all
be as happy as kings.*

by Robert Louis Stevenson

- Write the poem on the chalkboard.
- Read the poem. Explain that the author of the poem, Robert Louis Stevenson, wrote many poems and stories for children.
- Invite children to reread the poem with you and to share some of things they are happy about. List the items children name on the chalkboard.
- Talk about what we can do to help keep the world full of wonderful things. For example, replant trees to replace the ones we cut down; avoid littering to keep our lakes, rivers, and parks clean.
- Children will take a copy of this poem home on Home-School Connection Sheet 16.

Learn About Recycling

Core Activity

LITERACY OBJECTIVES

The child engages freely in conversation in varied situations; makes use of an environment rich in literacy materials.

MATERIALS

empty containers or trash that is ready to be thrown in the garbage, such as a jar, a soup can, or old clothing

- Display books such as *How Green Are You?* by David Bellamy (Potter, 1991) and *My First Green Book* by Angela Wilkes (Knopf, 1991).
- Involve children in a discussion about conservation and recycling. Make a list on the chalkboard of items that can be recycled, such as glass, aluminum, tin, paper, cardboard, and some kinds of plastic.
- Display items that are ready to be thrown out and ask children to brainstorm ideas about how the items might be used instead of discarded. For example, a jar could be used as a vase or a container for paint brushes; a large can could be used to hold buttons, crayons, or game pieces; old clothing could be cut into scraps for art projects or used for classroom clean-up.
- Encourage children to talk to their parents about reusing items and recycling newspapers, aluminum, and glass at home.

Dramatic Play

Implementing dramatic play centers

Let's Go Camping

Extended Time Activity

EQUIPMENT AND MATERIALS FOR CAMPING

tent, sheet, or blanket
sleeping bags or mats
flashlight
canteen or other water carrier
eating utensils
empty container for insect repellent
empty food containers
pots and pans
small cooler
pretend campfire

LITERACY MATERIALS

state and national parks brochures
travel brochures
journals for observations
pencils
directional signs and labels
campground signs
campsite maps
books and magazines
Blackline Master 3

Invite children to share any camping experiences they have had and talk about why people like to go camping. Have children decide what area of the room would be most suitable for a campsite and have them make suggestions about equipment that is needed. Write a list of equipment and supplies needed for a camping trip.

- Read *Gordon Goes Camping* by Julie Brinkloe (Doubleday, 1975) and *Bailey Goes Camping* by Kevin Henkes (Greenwillow, 1985).
- Show children camping equipment, such as a sleeping bag, flashlight, canteen or water carrier. Encourage them to think about how each piece of equipment is used and why it is needed.
- Provide state or national park brochures that show pictures and maps of camping areas and sites. Encourage children to discuss where they might like to camp, such as wooded, beach, or mountain areas.
- Provide a small tent or hang a sheet or a blanket over a rope strung across two corners of the room. Secure the corners of the blanket with rocks or blocks.
- Have children pantomime actions as you describe camping activities. *Wake up in the tent, stretch and yawn, unzip your sleeping bag and the tent zipper, start the fire, get water,* and so on.
- Encourage children to establish rules for the use of the center, such as *Only two campers in the tent.* Have children write and post the rules at the campsite.
- Invite children to think of a name for the campground and other signs, such as *Firewood Sold Here, Water,* or *Snack Shop.*

- Make a campfire by wrapping rolled newspapers in brown construction paper.
- Add crumpled red and orange paper to represent burning coals. Place a lighted flashlight in the center of the fire. Make a fire ring using rocks.
- Encourage campers to sing familiar songs around the campfire.
- Encourage children to use utensils and dishes from the housekeeping center to pretend to cook meals as they camp.
- Encourage campers to read books and magazines inside and outside the tent.
- Demonstrate writing in a camping journal, logging animals observed and meals cooked.
- Provide Blackline Master 3, Camping Checklist and Meal Planner.

Art

Creative extensions of the section topic

Make Recycled Art

Optional Activity

LITERACY OBJECTIVES
The child speaks in complete sentences; attends to others when they are speaking.

MATERIALS
recycled materials, glue, tape

- Display various recycled materials, such as bottle caps, string, ribbon, jar lids, washers, shoelaces, wrappers, sawdust, foam packing material, and so on. Ask children to name some of the items and tell how they were used.
- Invite children to choose any of the materials available, gluing them or taping them together, to create recycled art pieces.
- Encourage children to decide on names for their art pieces and to label them with the names.
- When the pieces have been titled, encourage children to introduce their art pieces to the class, explaining what they are made of and what they could be used for.

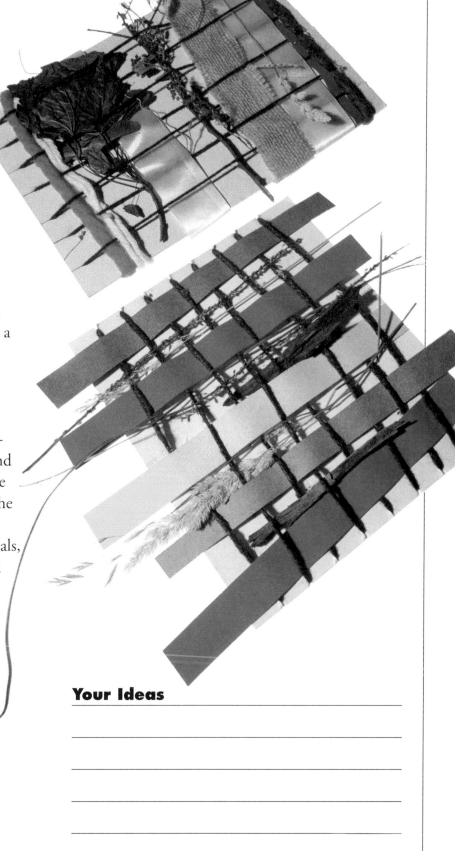

Make Nature Weavings

Extended Time Activity

LITERACY OBJECTIVE
The child follows oral directions.

MATERIALS
cardboard, yarn, ribbons, cloth strips, construction paper strips, grasses, leaves

- Take a walk outside and invite children to collect objects from nature, such as grasses, leaves, and twigs, that can be used to make a woven tapestry.
- Prepare a background for the weaving by making half-inch deep slits on the top and bottom edges of a cardboard rectangle.
- Tape the end of a piece of yarn to the backside of the cardboard. Wind the yarn around the cardboard, using the slits to stabilize the yarn. Secure the other end of the yarn on the back of the cardboard.
- Demonstrate how to weave recycled materials, paper strips, and natural materials over and under the yarn.
- Attach a ribbon or yarn to the top of the weaving so that it can be hung for display.

Your Ideas

_____

_____

_____

_____

_____

Music

Songs and activities related to the section topic

Is It Noise?

Extended Time Activity

LITERACY OBJECTIVE
The child discriminates environmental sounds appropriately.

MATERIALS
musical recordings, objects that make noise, bags

- Help children understand that when a noise is loud and unpleasant it is called noise pollution. Ask children to name some pleasant and unpleasant sounds as you list them on the chalkboard.
- Play recordings to demonstrate pleasant and soothing music.
- Give each child a bag and ask him/her to find something at home or in the classroom that makes an interesting noise, such as two spoons, pan lids, or an egg beater. Invite children to put the "instrument" in their bags without telling anyone what is inside.
- Encourage children to play their "instruments" for the class without letting the class see what is making the noise. Invite children to guess what the "instrument" is.
- Discuss each "instrument" played and ask children to decide if it is noise pollution or a pleasant sound.
- When each child has had a turn, play the "instruments" with a record.

Add Words to a Song

Optional Activity

LITERACY OBJECTIVES
The child matches spoken to printed words; knows that words are made of syllables.

MATERIALS
audiocassette tape Kindergarten Ecology– side 2 **KIT** *, chart paper, marker*

Fine Arts

"How To Be A Good Citizen"

- Listen to the song on the audiocassette tape.
- Write the words to the song on chart paper so that children can see the spoken-to-written word correspondence as you read the song together.
- Invite children to clap the beats or syllables of the words as the song is chanted.
- Have children think of other ways they can be good citizens, such as helping someone across the street or putting out a feeder for birds. Encourage children to sing about their ideas.

How To Be A Good Citizen

Across the Curriculum

Math, science, social studies, health activities

Count and Record Materials

Core Activity

LITERACY OBJECTIVE
The child writes in a variety of genres.

MATERIALS
Activity Sheets 15, Home-School Connection Sheet 16, recycled materials, pencils

Mathematics

• Encourage children to name materials they have thrown away in the past week.
• Have children bring empty plastic milk cartons, aluminum pop cans, and newspapers from home.
• Invite children to read Activity Sheet 15 with you, identifying each of the recycled materials being counted.
• Display the materials brought to school, have children count them, and record the number by placing Xs in the appropriate number of boxes.
• At the end of the week, have children check the *yes* or *no* box at the bottom of the page.
• On page 16, read the Home-School Connection with children so that they understand they'll be taking a walk and filling out the chart at home.

Make a Life Web

Core Activity

LITERACY OBJECTIVE
The child engages freely in conversation in varied situations.

MATERIALS
writing/drawing materials, yarn

Science

• Read stories such as *Once There Was a Tree* by Natalia Romanova (Dial Books, 1989) or *Anna's Rain* by Fred Burstein (Orchard Books, 1990), to initiate a discussion about the effect objects in the environment have on one another.
• Move outside to the playground and ask children to name objects in the environment, such as soil, grass, birds, plants, trees, and children, as you list them on a piece of paper.
• Return to the classroom and transfer the list of objects to the chalkboard.
• Encourage children to draw pictures of each object on cards, and write the name of the objects, using the list on the chalkboard as a model.
• Lay the cards on the floor and ask children to think about how objects in the environment are connected. Use yarn to connect each card to all other cards with which it interacts.
• Discuss the completed life web with children.

Adopt a Tree

Optional Activity

LITERACY OBJECTIVE

The child makes use of an environment rich in literacy materials.

MATERIALS

books containing pictures of and information about trees

Social Studies

- Read *A Tree is Nice* by Janice May Udry (Harper, 1956) or *Hello, Tree!* by Joanne Ryder (Lodestar, 1991) and discuss with children the ways a tree may be enjoyed.
- Talk about the ways in which trees are important to humans, animals, and our environment. Lead them to understand that trees not only beautify our planet, but help to keep it clean and healthy.
- Invite children to visit a nearby area where there are many trees and have each child choose a tree to adopt.
- Have children visit their trees throughout the year and participate in the following activities.

- Read a favorite story while relaxing next to the tree.
- Pick up litter near the tree.
- Draw a picture of the tree or make bark rubbings.
- Keep a diary of how the tree changes as the seasons change.
- Observe animals that live nearby the tree.
- Water the tree during dry weather.

Plant a City

Extended Time Activity

LITERACY OBJECTIVE

The child makes use of an environment rich in literacy materials.

MATERIALS

shoe boxes, playdough, craft sticks, nature magazines, scissors, glue, writing materials

Social Studies **Multicultural**

- Invite children to name different plants and animals found in areas in which they live.
- Display magazines that show plants and animals from environments around the world; for example, pictures of jungle vegetation and wildlife or desert cacti.
- Tell children they will be "planting" their own cities. Have pairs of children fill the bottom of shoeboxes with playdough.
- Encourage them to look through nature magazines and cut out pictures of plants and animals from around the world.
- Have children glue pictures to craft sticks.
- Have children "plant" their cities by pushing the ends of the craft sticks into the playdough.
- When the cities are completed, ask children to name their cities and write the names on the shoeboxes and share their cities with others.

Books to Enjoy

Books related to the section topic

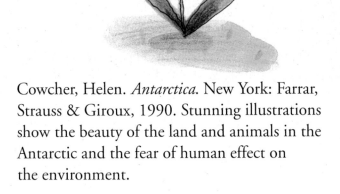

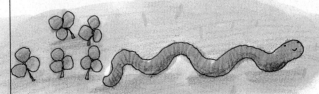

Arnosky, Jim. *In the Forest: A Portfolio of Paintings.* New York: Lothrop, 1989. The artist's sensitive paintings and text describe a forest setting.

Bellamy, David. *How Green Are You?* Il. by Penny Dann. New York: Clarkson Potter, 1991. This guide to taking care of our planet provides information and activities that promote conservation.

Brinkloe, Julie. *Gordon Goes Camping.* New York: Doubleday, 1975. As Gordon prepares to go camping, he finds that he'll need a friend to help him carry his supplies. Children can compare their own camping lists with Gordon's.

Burstein, Fred. *Anna's Rain.* Il. by Harvey Stevenson. New York: Orchard Books, 1990. Despite the rain and chill, Anna remembers to fill the birdfeeder and is thanked by the grateful birds.

Cowcher, Helen. *Antarctica.* New York: Farrar, Strauss & Giroux, 1990. Stunning illustrations show the beauty of the land and animals in the Antarctic and the fear of human effect on the environment.

Ehlert, Lois. *Color Farm.* New York: Lippincott, 1990. Bold colors and cutout shapes make this concept book a standout.

_____. *Feathers for Lunch.* San Diego: Harcourt, 1990. Paper cut-outs enhance this story of a cat who tries to catch wild birds, but ends up only with feathers.

Ets, Marie Hall. *Gilberto and the Wind.* New York: Viking, 1963. This "classic" can be read before going outdoors to experience the wind.

Florian, Douglas. *Nature Walk.* New York: Greenwillow, 1989. A family hiking on a nature trail discovers surprises in the woods.

Greeley, Valerie. *Where's My Share?* New York: Macmillan, 1989. This is a circular tale beginning with the baking of bread and ending with a robin looking for its share.

Henkes, Kevin. *Bailey Goes Camping.* New York: Greenwillow, 1985. Bailey wants to go camping with his rabbit scout siblings. His mother finds the perfect solution when she suggests that Bailey camp in the backyard.

Himmelman, John. *IBIS.* New York: Scholastic, 1990. A young whale who is caught in a fishing net is eventually released by concerned persons.

Kalan, Robert. *Rain.* Il. by Donald Crews. New York: Greenwillow, 1978. In this simple and direct book, the illustrator uses type to resemble a rainstorm before the rainbow.

Keller, Holly. *Will It Rain?* New York: Greenwillow, 1984. The animals in this fantasy get ready for a coming storm and then rejoice with the returning sun.

Parker, Mary Jessie. *City Storm.* Il. by Lynn Dennis. New York: Scholastic, 1990. The pastels in this book's illustrations look like the rain in the approaching storm.

Otto, Carolyn. *That Sky, That Rain.* New York: Harper, 1990. Readers will realize the goodness of rain as does the little girl in the story.

Romanova, Natalia. *Once There Was a Tree.* Il. by Gennady Spirin. New York: Dial Books, 1989. In this book about the passing of time and the laws of nature, a tree stump becomes a home to animals.

Ryder, Joanne. *Hello, Tree!* Il. by Michael Hays. New York: Lodestar Books, 1991. In this celebration of nature, a special tree not only provides shade and a place to climb, but becomes a familiar friend.

Udry, Janice May. *A Tree Is Nice.* New York: Harper, 1956. The Caldecott Medal winner reminds readers of the many ways trees can be enjoyed.

Wilkes, Angela. *My First Green Book: A Life-Size Guide to Caring for Our Environment.* New York: Knopf, 1991. A beautifully designed book with life-sized photographs of objects from nature.

Celebrating What We've Learned

Discuss Unit Celebration— Lead the Way to Earth Day

Core Activity

Celebrate the completion of the unit by inviting children and their families to lead the way to a schoolwide Earth Day Celebration. Brainstorm with children ideas on how to beautify the school, begin a recycling program, and promote conservation. In preparation for an Earth Day Celebration, have children draw and write about our beautiful earth, the seasons, and the weather. Have the group create an invitation asking family members to help them lead the way to Earth Day. In the invitation children can encourage family members to walk, ride bikes, take the bus, or car pool in the spirit of Earth Day conservation. Suggest that food for a picnic lunch be brought in reusable canvas bags, rather than paper, to help save a tree.

Promote Daily Conservation at School and Home

Invite children to create signs, posters, and pamphlets to promote conservation at school and at home, such as *Grow Plants to Help Clean the Air!* or *Carpool to Cut Down on Pollution!* Display them around the school during your Earth Day Celebration.

Beautify the School

Suggestions for beautifying your school include:

- Organizing and participating in a cleanup of litter around the school.
- Organizing a schoolwide cleanup of classrooms and hallways.
- Using biodegradable soaps to wash windows, floors, desks, walls, and playground equipment.
- Having parent volunteers repaint playground equipment or other parts of the school.
- Planting flowers around the building or in flowerboxes.
- Planting a tree or bushes.

Begin a Recycling Program

Kindergarten children can lead the way in a schoolwide recycling program by:

- Making posters to advertise recycling.
- Labeling recycling bins and placing in a central location of the school for recycling of glass, paper, aluminum, and plastic.
- Making flyers to send home to all families in the school about the recycling program.
- Preparing presentations for other classrooms to promote recycling.

Index

Acknowledgments

Text

Page 10: *The Bears' Autumn* by Keizaburo Tejima. Text and illustrations copyright © 1986 by Keizaburo Tejima. Reprinted by permission of Green Tiger Press, an imprint of Simon & Schuster Inc.

Page 29: "Different Days" from *Crackers & Crumbs* by Sonja Dunn. Reproduced with permission from Pembroke Publishers, 528 Hood Road, Markham, Ontario L3R 3K9.

Page 35: "What Shall We Do When We All Go Out?" from *Sharon, Lois & Bram's Mother Goose,* illustrated by Maryann Kovalski. Text copyright © 1985 by Grand Trunk Music. Reprinted by permission of Little, Brown, and Company.

Page 70: "Spring Rain" from *Around and About* by Marchette Chute. Copyright 1957 by E. P. Dutton, renewed © 1984 by Marchette Chute. Reprinted by permission of Elizabeth Roach.

Page 72: "Berry Picking" from *Poems for Small Friends* by Bobbi Katz. Text copyright © 1989 by Random House, Inc. Reprinted by permission of Random House, Inc.

Page 73: "Anti-Pollution Rap" from *Crackers & Crumbs* by Sonja Dunn. Reproduced with permission from Pembroke Publishers, 528 Hood Road, Markham, Ontario L3R 3K9.

Page 85: "How To Be A Good Citizen" from *Sniggles, Squirrels and Chicken Pox* by "Miss Jackie" Weissman. Copyright © 1984 by Jackie Weissman. Reprinted by permission.

Artist

G. Brian Karas, Cover, 1-96

Photographs

Joann Carney, Cover, 1, 7, 10, 12, 15, 19, 20, 25, 27, 28, 30, 34, 35, 36, 37, 40, 41, 42, 48, 49, 50, 52, 53, 56, 58, 59, 61, 62, 67, 69, 70, 76, 78, 80, 82, 83, 85, 90, 91, 93

Anthony Arciero, 2, 3, 6, 7, 8, 9, 10, 11, 12, 13, 16, 18, 19, 20, 21, 22, 23, 24, 26, 27, 32, 33, 35, 37, 38, 39, 40, 42, 43, 44, 45, 46, 47, 48, 49, 51, 54, 55, 58, 59, 63, 64, 65, 68, 74, 75, 79, 78, 83, 86, 87, 88, 89

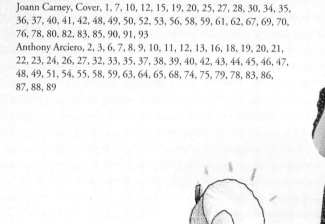

Joann   Brian   Anthony

Today's Weather   Date _____

City	Temperature
	○
_____	_____
	○
_____	_____
	○
_____	_____
	○
_____	_____

Conditions

Sunny

Cloudy

Partly
Cloudy

Rain

Snow

Flower Order Form

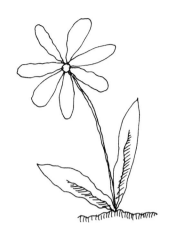

Name _____

Date _____

I want _____

_____

Deliver:

| Monday ☐ | Wednesday ☐ | Friday ☐ | Sunday ☐ |
| Tuesday ☐ | Thursday ☐ | Saturday ☐ | |

To:

From:

Have a Good Day!

From:

Happy Birthday!

From:

Camping Checklist

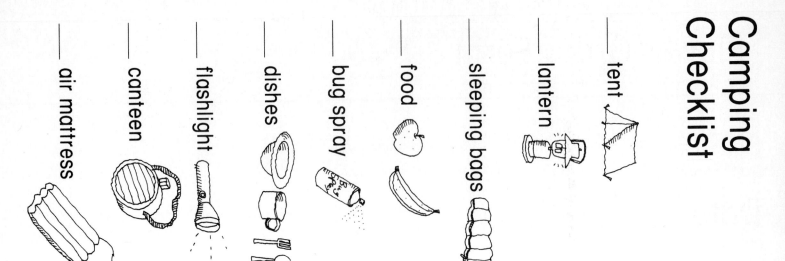

air mattress

canteen

flashlight

dishes

bug spray

food

sleeping bags

lantern

tent

Meal Planner	Monday	Tuesday
Wednesday	Thursday	Friday
Saturday	Sunday	